ORDER AND ANARCHY

Through the study of civil society, the evolution of social relations and the breakdown of social order, *Order and anarchy* re-examines the role of violence in human social evolution. Drawing on anthropology, political science and evolutionary theory, it offers a novel approach to understanding stability and instability in human society. Robert Layton provides a radical critique of current concepts of civil society, arguing that rational action is characteristic of all human societies and not unique to post-Enlightenment Europe. Case studies range from ephemeral African gold rush communities and the night club scene in Britain to stable hunter-gatherer and peasant cultures. The dynamics of recent civil wars in the former Yugoslavia, Chad, Somalia and Indonesia are compared to war in small-scale tribal societies. The author argues that recent claims for the evolutionary value of violence have misunderstood the complexity of human strategies and the social environments in which they are played out.

Robert Layton is Professor of Anthropology at the University of Durham. Recipient of the Royal Anthropological Institute's Rivers Medal for his research, Professor Layton has written widely on anthropological themes, including *The anthropology of art* (1991), *Australian rock art* (1992) and *An introduction to theory in anthropology* (1997).

ORDER AND ANARCHY

Civil society, social disorder and war

ROBERT LAYTON

CAMBRIDGE
UNIVERSITY PRESS

CAMBRIDGE
UNIVERSITY PRESS

University Printing House, Cambridge CB2 8BS, United Kingdom

One Liberty Plaza, 20th Floor, New York, NY 10006, USA

477 Williamstown Road, Port Melbourne, VIC 3207, Australia

314-321, 3rd Floor, Plot 3, Splendor Forum, Jasola District Centre, New Delhi - 110025, India

103 Penang Road, #05-06/07, Visioncrest Commercial, Singapore 238467

Cambridge University Press is part of the University of Cambridge.

It furthers the University's mission by disseminating knowledge in the pursuit of
education, learning and research at the highest international levels of excellence.

www.cambridge.org
Information on this title: www.cambridge.org/9780521674430

© Robert Layton 2006

First published 2006

A catalogue record for this publication is available from the British Library

Library of Congress Cataloging in Publication data
Layton, Robert, 1944–
Order and anarchy : civil society, social disorder and war / Robert Layton.– 1st ed.
p.   cm.
Includes bibliographical references and index.
ISBN-13 978-0-521-85771-0
ISBN-10 0-521-85771-6
ISBN-13 978-0-521-67443-0 (pbk.)
ISBN-10 0-521-67443-3 (pbk.)
1. Social stability.   2. Violence.   3. Social evolution.   4. Civil society.   I. Title.
HM896.L39   2006
303.6´2–dc22   2005029844

ISBN 978-0-521-85771-0 Hardback
ISBN 978-0-521-67443-0 Paperback

Contents

v

Acknowledgements

Warm thanks to all of the following for their helpful comments: Frances d'Souza; Chris Hann and Julia Eckert on chapter 1, Rob Aspden on chapter 2 and Elizabeth Chilton on chapter 4. The constructive editorial advice of the three anonymous readers has also helped immensely in making this a more readable book. Much of the library research was carried out while I was a Visiting Fellow at the Max Planck Institute for Social Anthropology in Halle, Germany, and I'm also grateful to Chris Hann's colleagues for their help and advice.

CHAPTER I

Civil society and social cohesion

INTRODUCTION

Background to the book

Order and anarchy grew out of several of my research interests. One originated in my doctoral research on social change in a cluster of French villages close to the Swiss border (see Layton 2000). I conducted several periods of fieldwork between 1969 and 1995, and relied on local archives to reconstruct continuity and change over a period extending back to the *ancien régime* that predated the French Revolution of 1789. The overwhelming impression I gained was that village life had remained remarkably orderly through a period that encompassed the 1789 Revolution, the agricultural revolution of the eighteenth and nineteenth centuries (associated with the turmoil of the enclosures in England), military occupations in the Franco-Prussian and Second World Wars, and the post-war mechanisation of agriculture. Knowing something about English village life, I was also impressed by the comparative vitality of local democracy and the freedom 'my' villages had to manage common pasture and forest. While I was analysing this material, however, state socialism in Eastern Europe was collapsing; sometimes in a more or less orderly fashion, elsewhere disintegrating into civil war. Political thinkers in both

Eastern and Western Europe saw the creation of 'civil society' in the Eastern bloc as the key to future political stability, and believed this would be facilitated by the development of a market economy. Through my involvement in the World Archaeological Congress, I also learned about the civil disorder in northern India that surrounded the 1992 destruction of the mosque at Ayodhya, which Hindu fundamentalists claimed stood on the site of a Hindu temple marking the birthplace of the culture hero Rama. The World Archaeological Congress met in India on the second anniversary of the mosque's destruction, and plans to debate the role of nationalist archaeologists in promoting the mosque's destruction were met by angry demonstrations. WAC deferred the debate and subsequently met in Croatia, where it was able also to examine the destruction of churches, mosques and other cultural property in the recent war between Serbia, Croatia and Bosnia (Layton, Stone and Thomas 2001). These experiences demanded a better understanding of the processes that sometimes allow society to change peacefully but at other times create violent conflict. Throughout the 1990s first-hand anthropological accounts of violence and civil war were accumulating, providing ways of investigating the topic in closer detail.

The argument

Order and anarchy is a study of civil society, of the construction and breakdown of social order and of the role of violence in human social evolution. 'Anarchy' has two meanings. It is generally understood to refer to the breakdown of authority in society, leading to social disorder. For Kropotkin and his fellow anarchists in later nineteenth-century Russia, however, it referred to the freedom of local communities to organise their lives through voluntary co-operation, the essence of civil society. Kropotkin actually visited the region in which my PhD research was conducted. He described how he drew inspiration from the voluntary associations he found among Swiss watchmakers: 'after a week's stay with the watchmakers, my views on socialism were settled. I was an anarchist' (Kropotkin 1972: 4). These opposed meanings reappear in recent debates about the definition of civil society. It is arguable whether the term 'civil society' can be applied to the institutions through which people pursue self-help and mutual aid against the state; the term is frequently confined to those non-governmental institutions that contribute to good order in the state.

Chapter 1 argues against restrictive definitions of civil society. It suggests the term can usefully be defined simply as 'social organisations occupying the space between the household and the state that enable people to co-ordinate their management of resources and activities'. The chapter argues against the view, proposed by Ernest Gellner (1994), Adam Seligman (1992) and Keith Tester (1992), that the capitalist market economy is uniquely conducive to the creation of civil society. It shows that John Locke and Adam Ferguson, the originators of the concept of civil society in the seventeenth and eighteenth centuries, regarded civil society as much more widely applicable, associating it with social co-operation based on rational self-interest in all human societies. Historical and recent non-Western examples are given in support of Locke's and Ferguson's position. Civil society may support or it may undermine the unity of the nation state, depending on historical circumstances. Chapter 1 traces the origin of current, restrictive characterisations of civil society to the political agendas of those who debated the English agricultural enclosures that took place between the sixteenth and early nineteenth centuries. It argues that the currently popular usage of

the term 'civil society' is unhelpful to the general understanding of social dynamics.

In the course of chapter 1, a number of salient theories
are introduced. Locke and his contemporaries are located in
the Enlightenment, when the divine right of kings was challenged, and philosophers encouraged rational debate concerning how human society should best be organised. During the
seventeenth century it was common practice to draw a contrast between the complex, seemingly contrived societies of
contemporary Europe and the supposed natural condition of
humanity. The difficulty was that no one had much idea what
that natural condition might have been. It was therefore generally viewed through the mirror of the type of society the
author sought to promote: as perpetual war or innocent peace.
A century later, writers such as Jean-Jacques Rousseau and
Adam Ferguson had better anthropological accounts to draw
on. The task of reconstructing the history of human society
assumed greater interest with the geological revolution of the
nineteenth century. Sudden understanding of the immense
period over which humanity had existed led writers to place
a series of intermediate stages between humankind's original
condition and modern European society. Social evolution was
held to move from the simple to the complex, and also from
superstition to rationality. It was this beguiling equation that
promoted more restrictive, idealistic notions of civil society.
Contemporary small-scale societies were equated with the earlier stages in the universal process. The theory of evolution as
progress was turned against English rural society during the
enclosures, decisively shaping recent understandings of civil
society. Even twentieth-century social scientists have found it
difficult to shake off the notion that evolution is progressive.
The sociologist Anthony Giddens, in rejecting evolutionary
approaches, characterises them as seeking a mechanism of
change that must be linked to a sequence of changes in which

types or aspects of social organisation replace each other across the whole spectrum of human history (Giddens 1984: 232).

This conception of evolution is utterly opposed to Charles Darwin's theory of natural selection, the theory that underpins biological scientists' approach to evolution. I shall argue that because Locke's work preceded the substantially misguided theory of evolution as progress, and because Ferguson stated it in an early and innocuous form, their ideas speak directly to current issues in Darwinian theory. Darwin argued that random variations between individuals in a population have different consequences for survival in a particular environment. Those individuals whose physiology or behaviour is best suited to the local environment will have a higher probability of surviving and producing viable children than will those bearing less appropriate variants. Adaptations are judged solely in relation to local conditions; no adaptation is universally 'better' or 'more evolved' than another. Even Darwin had difficulty grasping the inherent relativity of his model of natural selection and had to write to himself that 'I must not talk about higher and lower forms of life' (Trivers 1985: 32). If Darwinian hypotheses are applied to the analysis of human social behaviour they do not ask whether some forms of behaviour are intrinsically better than others, merely investigate how social strategies aid individuals' survival through social interaction in specific circumstances. After completing my PhD in 1971, I spent seven years in Australia working with Aboriginal communities. Traditional Aboriginal social life is adapted to survival in often harsh and unpredictable environments. I became interested in the work of socio-ecologists such as Bruce Winterhalder and Eric Alden Smith, who had used Darwinian theory to show how variations in human behaviour can be explained as adaptations to different environments and modes of subsistence. Socio-ecology offers a scientific explanation for uniformity and variation in the construction of social relations and will be relied upon at several points in the following analysis.

Chapter 2, 'Self-interest and social evolution', explores ways of applying a Darwinian approach to human social evolution. Chapter 2 contends that John Locke was right to argue that rationality is not a prerogative of Western civilisation, but characteristic of behaviour even in the simplest forms of social organisation. Game theory provides well-established models for exploring the rationality of social interaction in small groups, and I outline such key concepts as non-zero-sum games, the Prisoner's Dilemma, free-riding and ways of avoiding the Tragedy of the Commons.

The natural human condition is not, as Thomas Hobbes had claimed, one of perpetual war. The first part of the chapter gives ethnographic examples of the ways in which social order can be sustained in self-governing local communities, ranging from ephemeral gold rush communities to long-established villages. The second part argues that, since the breakdown of social order cannot be attributed to a natural human anarchy breaking free as the state loosens its grip, a more sophisticated theory of social order is needed. It draws on Darwinian theory to represent the evolution of social strategies, and the environments in which they are put into action, as a form of adaptation. A simplistic Darwinian model, which focuses only on the interaction of an organism and its environment, turns our attention away from the way that the interaction of individuals of different species, or people in different societies, can have cumulative effects on the ecology of individual behaviour. Chapter 2 therefore also introduces the concept of evolutionary 'fitness landscapes' to represent the cumulative effects of social interaction.

Chapter 3, 'The breakdown of social order', argues that if social order is to persist it must be economically sustainable.

Many recent ethnographic studies of social disorder implicate globalisation and 'structural adjustment' in the erosion
of the nation state's ability to fulfil its social contract with
citizens. Moreover, given the level of income created in the
market economy and the state's limited ability to collect tax
revenue, many Third World states cannot afford to sustain
the bureaucratic government they inherited from the colonial
era. Under such conditions, local civil society may offer better
security. The existing social order breaks down when changes
in the economic and social fitness landscape undermine the
effectiveness of previously dominant social organisations and
empower other strategies. Often these strategies already exist
as part of the local cultural repertoire. They include adherence
to kin and ethnic groups, feud and inter-ethnic violence. The
distribution of force may drift away from the state to become
concentrated in competing organisations within civil society.

The numerous cases of violent conflict in Europe, Africa
and Asia during the 1990s seem to show that contemporary society is increasingly vulnerable to apparently mindless acts of destruction. Hobbes's pessimism appears justified.
Chapter 4 looks carefully at this view, and criticises some of
the more deterministic applications of Darwinian theory to
human social behaviour. Evolutionary psychology, for example, argues that humans' capacity for social behaviour evolved
during the time we were hunter-gatherers and has sometimes
become inappropriate in the more complex societies of recent
times. Some authors have even concluded that humans share
a genetic disposition to violence with chimpanzees, and that
culture provides an inadequate safeguard. Chapter 4 therefore
looks at evidence for the evolutionary significance of human
warfare. It argues that warfare and peacemaking are equally
important in human social evolution. The chapter highlights
common characteristics in tribal warfare and civil war within

nation states that arise from the pursuit of competing strategies in situations where resources are scarce, trust under threat
yet the means to violence prevalent.

Characterising civil society

In the work of influential recent writers such as Ernest Gellner
(1994) and Adam Seligman (1992), the concept of 'civil society'
is central to the analysis of stability and instability in the nation
state. As the post-Second World War socialist regimes of Eastern Europe began to crumble, there was widespread optimism
about the ability of people to come together to promote a common interest in self-determination, in democracy, through the
medium of civil society. Western governments who aided the
dismantling of socialism contended that a free market economy
promoted self-reliance, and thus participation in civil society.
The alleged absence of civil society under socialism was taken
as proof of its intrinsic connection with capitalism. During the
next few years, however, faith in the universal development
of civil society was shaken by events such as the rise of ethnic nationalism in former Yugoslavia. Whether civil society
could be said to exist in such cases was questioned. Relationships based on kinship and ethnicity appeared categorically
opposed to those underpinning civil society; they seemed, in
Adam Seligman's (1992) terms, primordial, not rational. A
number of questions are therefore addressed in the first part
of the chapter.

- How should 'civil society' be defined?
- Is civil society necessarily associated with a commercial
  economy (as Gellner and Seligman argue) or can it occur
  under different regimes (as Hann and White contend)?
- Does civil society necessarily tend to support or undermine
  the state?

In the second part of the chapter I review what John Locke (1632–1704) and Adam Ferguson (1723–1816) actually wrote about civil society, showing that they intended the concept to have much wider application than its current usage. The third part of the chapter therefore explores how the current, circumscribed and politically biased approach originated and how alternative, equally useful approaches have been marginalised.

The Enlightenment concept of civil society was first formulated by Locke (1960 [1689]) and Ferguson (1995 [1767]). During the mid-1980s, political scientists in both Eastern and Western Europe advocated creating a civil society in Eastern Europe as a way of pushing back the state (Hann 1990; Khilnani 2001). The fact that the concept of civil society was coined during the period when Western European society was undergoing the great transformation from feudalism to mercantile capitalism was considered decisive by analysts writing in the 1990s. Because the concept was invented at the time when the divine right of kings was challenged, and the new bourgeoisie pressed for the abolition of feudal social order, it was assumed that civil society itself was born at that time.

The anthropologist and political philosopher Ernest Gellner (who died in 1995) was a true child of the Enlightenment, convinced of the unique rationalism of European culture since the birth of mercantile capitalism. He grew up in Prague, but emigrated with his parents to England in 1939. After the fall of communism in Eastern Europe, he returned to Prague to promote the particular type of civil society associated with a market economy. According to Gellner, only a market economy ensures that contractual associations are sufficiently flexible and adaptive to create civil society (Gellner 1994: 100). Market society allows the individual to enter and leave specific-purpose, limited associations without elaborate blood ritual. (Gellner parodies the structure of traditional societies.) Only the market promotes the rational pursuit of self-interest, or what Gellner (77) curiously calls 'a disinterested pursuit of interest'. Many in Eastern Europe were at first willing to accept this claim. Given the sudden abandonment of communism people were, as Janine Wedel (1998) writes, looking for quick answers to the problem of preserving social cohesion. The only alternative seemed the Western capitalism advocated by international agencies.

Recent proponents of civil society have argued for a narrow definition that fails to do justice to the breadth of vision of the concept's originators. As Steven Sampson discovered, Western models do not always match Eastern realities; procedures cannot be exported successfully if their institutional social framework is absent. Problems that are solved in the West by commercial or voluntary associations are often solved by kin, local networks and ethnic groups in other societies (Sampson 1996: 125). In the post-Soviet era, millionaire/billionaire former communists and other Russians have searched in vain for a bourgeoisie committed to democracy, productive economic behaviour and civil society (Kingston-Mann 2003: 94). Mass privatisation in Russia did not create civil society, but profit-seeking oligarchs and gangsters who hired private armies and intelligence-gathering teams, and perpetrated frequent car-bombings and contract murders (Kingston-Mann 2003: 109).

DEFINING CIVIL SOCIETY

The sociologist Alvin Gouldner characterised civil society as a medium through which people 'can pursue their own projects in the course of their everyday lives; and as ways of avoiding dependence on the domination of the state . . . [through] patterns of mutual and self-help' (Gouldner 1980: 370–1). Elizabeth Dunn (1996: 27) describes civil society as 'the domain of relationships which falls between the private realm of the family on the one hand and the state on the other'. Since the household is virtually universal in human societies I shall use 'civil society' to refer specifically to *social organisations occupying the space between the household and the state that enable people to co-ordinate their management of resources and activities.*[1]

Civil society and the state in Europe

Since civil society exists between the domains of state and household, institutions that only promote state policy are not civil institutions; they are part of the state. A particular institution may therefore have civic capability at some times, but not others, depending on the relative power of the state. In France the mayor plays a dual role, both representing the state and implementing local civil society. The contemporary structure of French local government was laid down at the time of the Revolution of 1789, embodying the conflicting policies of the Revolutionary government toward local democracy and a unified state (Abélès 1991: 111, 115). Since 1871, the village council has chosen the mayor from among its own members. In the internal affairs of the commune (village), the mayor is the agent of the council and obliged to put the council's decisions into effect. The mayor thus has a dual role, representing both the state and local civil society. In the part of Franche Comté where I worked (Layton 2000), communes earned between half a million and one million francs a year through the sale of timber from communal forests during the 1990s, and the municipal council has significant resources at its disposal to fund local public services.

[1] I am aware that establishing the boundaries of the household can be problematic (see Layton 2000: 124).

Brian Chapman (1953) recorded the case of a mayor who, in response to pressure from his councillors, banned the carriage and use of nuclear weapons within his commune. Winnie Lem (1999) has documented the subversive activities of mayors in the Languedoc region of France, where there is a century-old history of regional resistance to state centralisation. Even the mayor participates in the 'hidden economy' in order to avoid paying state-imposed taxes and insurance.

In France, a degree of local autonomy in civil society is tolerated. Susanne Spülbeck (1996), on the other hand, reports that the mayor of the East German village she studied was arrested in the late 1950s, during the socialist regime, and charged with political conspiracy. No villagers were willing to take over, and the post was filled by outsiders for more than ten years. Although the post of mayor has been well paid since the collapse of socialism, and the political system is more liberal, it is still very difficult to recruit a mayor. State surveillance has left a crushing mark upon local civil society.

Function and history

The consequences of civil activities should be studied empir-ically. One cannot include in the definition a moral require-ment that civil society function to support or oppose the state, nor that it should exclusively promote individual liberty or group cohesion. Gellner considers, but then rejects, a defini-tion of civil society that specifies its role in relation to the state. He suggests civil society might be:

That set of diverse non-governmental institutions which is strong enough to counterbalance the state and, while not preventing the state from fulfilling its role of keeper of the peace and arbiter between major interests, can nevertheless prevent it from dominating and atomising the rest of society. (Gellner 1994: 5)

Gellner rejects a definition of this type because it would include 'many forms of social order which would not satisfy *us*' (Gellner 1994: 6, his emphasis). He argues there must be no segmentary tendencies in civil society because, if there are, civil society will fragment the state, not counterbalance it. His argument pre-empts the study of how civil society works in particular cases.

Seligman points out that Eastern and Western arguments for civil society differ due to the *contradictory* aspirations of its modern proponents. This ambivalence is clear in Gellner's essay, as his former colleague Jack Goody (2001: 153) has pointed out: for Gellner civil society must always be 'on the side of the angels'. Gellner (1994) shifts his evaluation of civil society, depending on whether he is writing of the West or Eastern Europe. In the West, he argues, the state must restrain the power of the market economy. The state can be trustworthy in the West. Profits often accrue to 'smart-alecks' who manipulate the market with dubious legitimacy. There must be some form of welfare state, because the household is too small to look after the disabled. Similarly the state must be responsible for the provision of many services. 'If socialism means that political constraints are put on the economy, then virtually all ... societies ... are socialist' (Gellner 1994: 170, cf. Seligman 1992: 113–17). On the other hand, Gellner argues, the market economy in Eastern Europe is too weak to create a genuine civil society; in Eastern Europe, it is civil society that must develop to counterbalance the state, not the other way round. I argue that, before discussing the functions of civil society, one must investigate empirically what institutions lie between households and state, in other words, what framework exists to enable members of different households to take joint action. It is then possible to ask which (if any) of these institutions enable people to promote their political aims. *If* civil society tends to undermine the state, the identity of the coalitions that replace the state are likely to depend on the structure of such intermediate institutions.

The concept of civil society also needs to be freed from the evolutionist assumption that it emerges within the social life of the state at some particular point in the state's evolution, particularly the point at which commercial capitalism dissolves traditional local communities (e.g. the period of the English enclosures). There are two weaknesses in this approach. It wrongly implies people were previously incapable of coming together rationally, to pursue their mutual self-interest. It also tends to imply, misleadingly, that the structure or extent of civil society is coincident with that of the state. 'A sphere of society distinct from the state and with forms and principles of its own' (Kumar 1993: 376) may precede the state (particularly in the case of colonially created states), or may cut across state boundaries (Kurdish society, for example). Complaining that these cases do not constitute civil society amounts to saying 'they do not engage with the state in the way I believe civil society should'. Jack Goody (2001) demonstrates the ethnocentric bias in much recent Western work on civil society, citing forms of civil society in ancient India, Tang and Sung China and pre-colonial West Africa.

Chris Hann (2003) expresses surprise that Gellner, an anthropologist, should reject the possibility of civil society in a tribal or an Islamic society. Hann argues that a properly anthropological approach would look more closely at local patterns of sociality and investigate how issues of political and moral accountability can be resolved in civil ways that differ from modern Western solutions. Sami Zubaida (2001) reviews the variety of forms of civil society in the contemporary Middle East. The most astonishing aspect of Gellner's study is the way it parodies traditional society. According to

Gellner, pre-modern states often lacked the means to pulverise the societies they controlled. But the cost, he asserts, is that the peasant falls under the tyranny of the local community, of cousins and ritual. The historical evidence from European villages summarised below shows this claim to be simplistic.

The simple layered model presented above ('social organisations occupying the space between the household and the state') may be misleading if it is visualised as an inverted triangle with the all-encompassing state at the top, and the smallest component unit, the household, at the bottom. A civil institution may extend throughout the state (e.g. Polish Solidarity), and the state generally penetrates down to the local level (e.g. the village mayor in his role as state functionary). The state also frequently sets the rules for civil associations such as producer co-operatives, even though such associations are freely established and promote free association in pursuit of their members' local goals.

'Civil society' is, as Krishan Kumar (1993) shows, a term that has been used in various ways by different schools of political philosophy. Kumar concludes that the term has no neutral social-scientific meaning. I argue that the term is useful, but on two conditions. First, the structure of civil society must be distinguished from the various functions it may perform in different times and places. A particular case should not be excluded from the category 'civil society' merely because the writer finds its social consequences undesirable. Second, civil society should not be equated with an alleged stage in the evolution of society.

Must civil society engage with the state?

While there is a strong case for rejecting ethnocentric definitions of civil society that specify the role it should play, the question, 'must the institutions of civil society play, by definition, some political role toward the state?' is harder to answer. Wedel describes the Western goal of creating civil society in Eastern Europe after the collapse of the socialist regimes as one 'in which citizens and groups are free to form organisations that functioned independently of the state *and that mediated between citizens and the state*' (Wedel 1998: 83, my emphasis). Empirical ethnographic research suggests that particular institutions may play a political role at some points in their existence, but not others. I think it would be unhelpful to exclude such institutions from analysis except when they move into the political arena. One needs to know how they originated, and what circumstances prompted their members to transform their function so as to use them as a vehicle for political action. A classic example is Bill Epstein's (1958) study of how a missionary-founded library association in the Zambian mining township of Luansha was transformed into a Welfare Society that, in turn, provided rising Black leaders with the vehicle to challenge the urban authority of tribal elders. Alexis de Tocqueville (1805–59), the nineteenth-century French political theorist, travelled to the United States in 1831 and later wrote on the nature of democracy. De Tocqueville's distinction between political institutions and civil institutions is helpful (cited Kumar 1993: 381); civil associations such as churches, professional, commercial and recreational associations can 'pave the way' for political association. To avoid classifying particular institutions as necessarily political *or* civil, it may be more useful to say that civil associations have some autonomy to manage resources and co-ordinate action, and therefore have the *potential* to advance their members' political interests in dialogue with the state.

Seligman claims civil society did not exist under socialism, since the civil and political elements were denied (Seligman 1992:114). Michał Buchowski disputes the claim that no civil society existed in Central Europe during the communist era (Buchowski 1996: 79, cf. Wedel 1998: 103). True, communist ideology sought to merge the state and society. The *nomenklatura* system ensured only loyal people could hold the most significant posts. Nonetheless, people followed their own interests through official associations created and licensed by the state. As a teenager in Poland, Buchowski argues, he was contributing to building a civil society when he belonged to a People's Sports Club and played football. He was, in other words, contributing to social organisations occupying the space between the household and the state that enable people to co-ordinate their management of resources and activities. Other state-sponsored organisations such as village women housekeepers' associations and volunteer fire brigades provided similar scope. Senior posts had to be approved by the party, and ordinary members were expected to respect authority. But such associations provided a significant means for collective activity and many, especially professional organisations, transformed themselves into dissident bodies in the 1980s.

Is civil society segmentary or unifying?

Case studies demonstrate that civil society may threaten or support the unity of the nation state. Where the state threatens to break down into smaller polities it is inadequate to characterise ethnic or religious affiliation as 'primordial', that is 'innate and irrational' (Duffield 2001: 110). A comparison of the recent history of Yugoslavia and Poland makes this clear. Ethnic communities created fault lines in the Yugoslavian state. In some regards they predated the state into which they were incorporated and their persistence weakened the state, but the divisions that existed in 1990 were not 'primordial'. Their survival was due to covert recognition by the state and their character had been transformed by their interaction with the state. Serbia and Croatia have a long history as separate political entities. The medieval kingdom of Serbia was founded in the sixth century AD and lasted until its defeat by the Ottoman Turks in 1389. Ottoman rulers allowed the Serbs to continue practising Orthodox Christianity, which therefore functioned as an expression of Serb identity in a predominantly Islamic state. Three small Croatian states existed in the eighth century. During this period Charlemagne brought Croatia into the Catholic Church. The Croatian kingdoms were unified in 1069, but Croatian independence was short-lived. Only thirty years later Croatia was defeated by Hungary. Croatia agreed to a union with Hungary but Croatia's political identity was preserved by the *Sabor*, or Croatian assembly, which continued to exist until the end of the Austro-Hungarian Empire in 1918 (Tanner 1997). Because Catholicism was shared with the wider Empire, it was not structurally significant as a defining institution of Croat identity, which was expressed through the *Sabor*.

After the First World War, southern Slav unity was achieved with the creation of Yugoslavia. Unfortunately, the unified state suffered from a fatal asymmetry. Serbia gained independence from Turkish rule before Croatia ceased to be part of the Austro-Hungarian Empire. Serbs dominated the new state institutions and Croatia lost the relative autonomy it had exercised through the *Sabor*. Ethnic rivalry was therefore encouraged and Catholicism now became a salient aspect of Croat identity. After the Second World War ethnicity and nationalism persisted because Tito, the president of post-Second World War Yugoslavia, created an ethnically based federal structure without genuine power sharing. During the second half of the twentieth century, ethnic identity became irrelevant for many city dwellers, but it remained strong in the countryside. 'Pan-Yugoslav consciousness [cf. Gellnerian civil society] existed and there is evidence it was growing in the 1980s but it proved too weak' to overcome ethnic conflict (Gallagher 1997: 48). After Tito's death, communist elites in both Serbia and Croatia embraced ethnic nationalism to ensure their survival, but those nationalist leaders had to draw their support from rural communities. Intermarriage and even contact with other communities occurred much less frequently in the countryside, and villagers were 'ready to take up arms against cities as mythical places of affluence and sin' (Gallagher 1997: 66). Tom Gallagher concludes that it is only a slight exaggeration to describe the conflict of the 1990s as one between urban (tolerant) and rural (nationalist) communities, expressed through a religious idiom.

Poland, on the other hand, was fortunate in having civil institutions that extended throughout the country, exemplifying the point that the institutions of civil society are not necessarily less inclusive than the state. The position of the Catholic Church in Poland was unique in Eastern and Central Europe. In contrast to the divisive effect of churches in Yugoslavia, the Polish Catholic Church was an emblem of national unity. The communists could neither destroy it nor use it for their own ends. It represented the interests of various groups at various levels. Through its preaching it maintained freedom of speech. After martial law was imposed in 1981, churches became 'safe havens' for secular dissidents (Kumar 1993, Buchowski 1996). The Catholic Church therefore played a practical role in promoting a national civil society.

Unmodern civil society

Modernity has been used as a broad synonym for the era of capitalism. Traditional loyalties to local communities were broken up by the mass movement of workers in search of employment, medieval traditions were discarded as irrational superstitions, and the Enlightenment vision of universal reason inspired attempts at planned intervention in the order of society. Gellner's vision of civil society is a modernist one, according to which only a market economy guarantees flexible contractual associations and voluntary specific-purpose associations. Gellner also perpetuates the modernist conflation of pre-modern European societies (i.e. approximately pre-eighteenth century) and recent, non-industrial societies (cf. Fabian 1983).

The historical evidence from European villages shows Gellner is incorrect to claim that civil society did not exist in the Middle Ages. In 1483, the Swiss village of Torbel already referred to itself as a peasant corporation when it laid down rules for the use of common pasture and forest it owned (Netting 1981: 60). In the fifteenth and sixteenth centuries the citizens of Torbel drew up charters stating that, while villagers might sell their own strips of plough land to outsiders, they could not transfer their rights in common land. New members could join the village if two-thirds of its existing members agreed. Before 1790, French village affairs were regulated by popular assemblies and officers appointed by seigneurs or local government (Gournay, Kesler and Siwek-Pouydessau 1967: 115). In the French alpine village of Abriès all household heads who held taxable land, including widows, had the right to attend the pre-Revolutionary assembly. The assembly elected consuls to represent its interests before higher courts, and used communal funds earned from leasing pasture to employ teachers and lawyers. In 1694, an army engineer wrote: 'these people govern themselves like Republicans not recognizing any leader among them nor having to suffer any nobility' (Rosenberg 1988: 39). Village corporations clearly occupied part of the space between household and state.

Gellner (1994: 88) contends that in 'the days of' clans and lineages, you could not readily change your membership of a local group, preventing individuals from entering or leaving specific-purpose, limited associations (see above). It is simply impossible to generalise on this scale. Anthropological research shows bands, lineages and clans are all to some degree flexible in membership. Richard Lee wrote that the Dobe !Kung (Ju/'hoansi) hunter-gatherers of the Kalahari desert 'move from camp to camp with distressing frequency; some alternate among two or more waterholes . . . others move right out of the Dobe area several times a year or for years at a time' (Lee 1979: 42). Particular clusters of people have a history of association with one waterhole varying from a few years to several decades but, according to Lee, it rarely extends back to the grandparental generation of the oldest living people. Individuals may choose whether to join their mother's or father's band. Such flexibility is essential for hunter-gatherers living in an unpredictable environment subject to local drought. Descent groups among pastoralists and subsistence farmers seem more durable, but M. Glickman (1971) and Michel Verdon (1982) demonstrated that lineages among the cattle-herding Nuer of the southern Sudan absorb non-kin who have lived in the village long enough to become accepted as members, while former lineage members who move away are forgotten. Gunter Schlee (2002) describes the Somali clan system as one in which the weak seek to attach themselves to the powerful. If the lineage model cannot embrace them, he writes, they can be attached by contract. The primary consideration governing the durability of social relations is whether individuals need to invest in social access to resources for a long-term return. The hunter-gatherers of the Kalahari invest in wide-ranging social networks that allow them to move from band to band, thus avoiding the risk of local drought and violence. Peasants, and even swidden cultivators, invest in land and crops, while pastoralists invest in collective rights over herds. Contract-based industrial employment renders this kind of investment of social groups unnecessary and, if dispossessed of land, impossible. People do not suddenly acquire a rational civic consciousness; shifts in access to resources dictate different social strategies.

Gellner retreats to some extent from his rigid characterisation of pre-modern society when he discusses Islam. Following Ibn Khaldun, he notes that rural communities had some independence from the centre, and could periodically reform urban decay. The rural hinterland provided 'a kind of political womb of cohesive communities, well able and indeed obliged to defend and administer themselves: these could also run a larger state when given the chance by the decline of a previous dynasty. The state was a gift of the tribe to the city' (Gellner 1994: 84). However, Gellner also contends that, since tribes are not equipped to run a bureaucracy, 'society is ruled by networks, quasi-tribes, alliances forged on the basis of kin, services exchanged, common regional origin . . . still, in general, based on personal trust . . . rather than on . . . a defined bureaucratic structure' (27).

Jenny White (1996) challenges Gellner's view that civil society must be based on contract. White agrees that 'In urban Turkey, voluntary associations, grass-roots protest actions and other forms of civic activities often are organized on the basis of mutual trust and interpersonal obligation, rather than on an individual, contractual membership basis. Trust and reciprocity characterize communal life in general' (White 1996: 143). But, she insists, civic action is *not* today based on 'primordial' ties of clan, tribe or family. It is created through the free choices of individuals, who decide whom to associate with among their acquaintances and in their community. This network creates a space in which women can act publicly without leaving the privacy and security of communal and gendered roles. The web of already existing community ties is the foundation of a civic culture upon which both Islamic and secular groups build organisational infrastructures among the working class.

Sami Zubaida (2001) looks more critically at civil society in the Middle East, agreeing with White that the traditional associations in the Middle East have been reconstituted under modern conditions as tribal, religious and village associations in cities, but conceding that urban civil society in the Middle East has strong illiberal tendencies (Zubaida 2001: 242).

Hann argues that the ethnocentric definition of civil society relied on by Western agencies damaged the way assistance was provided to post-socialist regimes in Eastern Europe. Communities that had just endured a massive experiment in social engineering under socialism were then subjected to an equally idealistic experiment in social engineering inflicted upon them by foreigners. A specifically Western concept of civil society, based on contractual associations and individual agents, was exported to people who may prefer their own traditional associations. The positive aspects of socialist government—state support for pensions, education or health—are lost, but nothing is put in their place. 'Huge numbers of postsocialist citizens feel they enjoyed a more civil society under the old regime than they do today' (Hann, personal communication). Hann suggests the effect of Western intervention may even be to strengthen loyalties based on kinship, religious or ethnic identity in reaction to the crudities and abuses of the foreign NGO sector.

LOCKE AND FERGUSON: THE ORIGINS OF THE CONCEPT OF 'CIVIL SOCIETY'

Political thought during the Enlightenment

Until the seventeenth and eighteenth centuries, European kings had been believed to rule by divine right, and human society was supposed to reproduce, on a lower scale, the divine society of Heaven. These assumptions were questioned during the Enlightenment, when philosophers rejected divine law and appealed to human reason to deduce how society should best be organised. Once people considered themselves free to decide for themselves what was, or was not, proper social behaviour it became possible to ask both how actual societies might be improved, and how present societies had diverged from the natural or original human condition. Both the European past and more exotic, but living, human societies were seen as sources of information that could help answer these questions.

Thomas Hobbes (1588–1679), who was at one time tutor to the future King Charles II, experienced the disorder caused by the English Civil War at first hand and asked what it was that holds a society together. Hobbes envisaged the opposite condition to centrally regulated social life as one of random disorder, in which people sought their own self-preservation by trying to control others. Such a condition would be a war of every man against every other man, and life would be 'solitary, poore, nasty, brutish and short' (Hobbes 1970 [1651]: 65). Hobbes imagined that people living in such a condition would therefore be compelled to choose a leader, or sovereign, and surrender sufficient of their personal freedom to the sovereign to give him the power he needed to uphold a social contract. People would only be willing to work for the general good if they could be confident that anyone cheating would be punished by law. Hobbes's main aim was to construct a logical opposition between order and disorder, rather than to identify an actual condition against which contemporary European society could be assessed (Hill 1958: 271).

The philosopher John Locke (1632–1704) argued that people possessed 'natural rights' that they were entitled to defend against an oppressive state. Implicitly directed against Hobbes, Locke's overt target was Robert Filmer (d. 1635), who championed the divine right of kings and traced the origin of royal authority to the power a father held over his family in 'primitive times'. Locke countered that women are not naturally subjugated to men. Marriage is a contract made for the purpose of raising children and either partner has the right to withdraw. 'Men living together according to reason, without a common Superior on Earth with Authority to judge between them, is *properly the state of nature*' (Locke 1960: 280, his emphasis).

Hobbes and Locke had little empirical evidence to support their reconstructions of the natural human condition. Eighteenth-century writers had more reports to draw upon, particularly descriptions of native society in the Caribbean and North America. Jean-Jacques Rousseau (1712–78), a diplomat and citizen of Geneva during the last years of the feudal *ancien régime*, imagined humankind had probably originated as solitary individuals, satisfying their meagre wants immediately, but rarely, if ever, coming into contact with one another. He noted that contemporary peoples in the Caribbean appeared to have no concept of private property or market exchange. Rousseau guessed that people formed an association when natural sources of food began to be depleted and people turned to agriculture; banding together to defend their tilled land against others who wanted to annex it. 'All ran headlong to

their chains, in the hopes of securing their liberty'(Rousseau
1963 [1755]: 205). The Scottish social philosopher Adam
Ferguson (1723–1816) more perceptively understood that
humans are intrinsically social. He countered that a wild man
caught in the woods is no more representative of humanity's
original state than an eye that has never seen anything. A wild
man would probably be as defective as an organ that had never
performed its intended function.

Adam Seligman (1992) and Keith Tester (1992), writing
on civil society in the wake of the collapse of East European
socialism, have misrepresented the way the concept was first
formulated in Locke's *Two treatises of government* (1689) and
Ferguson's *An essay on the history of civil society* (1767). Neither
Locke nor Ferguson claimed civil society was a new phenomenon. Tester, on the other hand, gives what he describes
as a simple or even simplistic definition of civil society: civil
society is the milieu of private contractual relations; relations
that go beyond the family, yet are not of the state. He concludes
that 'civil' is implicitly opposed to 'barbaric'. Civil society is
made by civilising social relationships. Other, non-Western
societies were therefore, by definition, uncivil (Tester 1992:
8–10). Tester is perpetuating the nineteenth-century notion
of progressive social evolution. He is right to point out that
Locke's representation of contract as the basis of human society universalises the bourgeois property holder (Locke 1960:
288, Tester 1992: 44). But this does not justify going to the
other extreme and asserting that people have no freedom
to enter into or leave social relationships in pursuit of their
self-interest in societies other than those built on commercial
capitalism.

Seligman contends that the idea of civil society emerged
during the seventeenth and eighteenth centuries in response to
a social crisis, and has re-emerged in the late twentieth century

in response to another crisis (Seligman 1992: 15). Seligman argues that in the seventeenth century the commercialisation of land, labour and capital, and growth of the market economy, led political theorists to replace the notion of binding traditions with that of a social contract. Seligman, like Gellner, therefore dates the origin of civil society to that time. The discovery of non-Western societies where life was organised differently also called into question the 'naturalness' of European social life. Tester is correct to point out that the question, 'what holds society together?' was a particularly pertinent one in Europe during the period the divine right of kings was rejected, and commercial capitalism overturned feudalism. But Locke's and Ferguson's interests were wider than an attempt to understand the unique condition of 'modernity'. Contrary to Tester's claim, that was not the first time 'the voluntary associations of independent, mannered and civilised individuals were actually occurring' (Tester 1992: 125), and nor do Locke or Ferguson suppose it was (further examples of pre-seventeenth-century contractual relationships are given below).

Locke's sociological method, shared with Thomas Hobbes and Jean-Jacques Rousseau, was to discover the natural human condition. Once the supposed natural condition had been established, the condition in which people actually live could be measured against this reference point. Locke wrote his *Two treatises* to refute Filmer's argument that the natural social condition was one of 'patriarchal authority' in which kings could trace their power to Eve's original subjugation to Adam. Locke argued the contrary. 'We are born free, as we are born rational' (Locke 1960: 95). The liberty of acting according to our own will, not from compulsion by the will of others, is grounded on the possession of reason (309). Unlike Hobbes and Rousseau, Locke recognised that humans are intrinsically social. The natural condition is a social one. 'The *first Society* was between

man and wife' (Locke 1960: 318–19, emphasis in original).
Contrary to Seligman's representation (Seligman 1992: 22),
Locke clearly thought that contracts exist in the state of nature.
The marriage contract is made *either* by the partners them-
selves 'in the state of Nature, *or* by the Customs or Laws of the
Country they live in' (1960: 321, my emphasis). According to
Locke, the state of nature has two distinctive characteristics.
First, people rely on self-help, rather than appeal to delegated
authorities, to defend their property. Second, parties to a con-
tract formulate the terms of the agreement among themselves.
Locke clearly considered civil society to be an aspect of the
natural human condition (contrary to Laslett 1960: 107–8 and
Seligman 1992: 22). Adam Ferguson, as we have seen, also
took the view that humans are intrinsically social. 'Mankind
are to be taken in groupes, as they have always subsisted'
(Ferguson 1995: 10). Like Locke, Ferguson did not confine
reason or civil society to mercantile capitalism.

   For Locke, the natural condition ends and *political* society comes into being when people surrender their right of
self-help 'into the hands of the community'. The community
'comes to be Umpire, by settled standing rules, indifferent,
and the same to all parties; and by Men having Authority
from the Community, for the execution of these rules' (Locke
1960: 324). The community now sets the terms of contractual
agreements. Those who belong to a particular political society share a common law and recognise the same authorities to
resolve disputes (324). It is absolutely clear that Locke does
not regard civil society as something that had recently come
into existence. Equally, the state of nature is an ever-present
possibility: 'Want of a common Judge with authority, puts all
Men in a State of Nature' (Locke 1960: 281). ''Tis plain the
World never was, nor ever will be, without numbers of Men
in that State' (276).

Locke defined property as a resource that has been taken from the state of nature and improved by labour (Locke 1960: 288). Locke's account may misleadingly suggest he associated the origin of property with the enclosure movement (that regarded common land as unowned) and therefore something that originated in his own time (see Laslett's editorial footnote to Locke 1960: 288). But Locke recognises that foragers can own property: 'He that is nourished by the Acorns he pickt up under an Oak, or the Apples he gathered from the Trees in the Wood, has certainly appropriated them to himself' (288). Locke is not wide of the mark: Lorna Marshall (1976) wrote that among the !Kung (Ju/'hoansi) of the Kalahari the person whose arrow first wounds a game animal is obliged to distribute the meat among households in camp. However, meat once distributed and vegetable foods once gathered become private property. One man was killed for stealing honey from a bees' nest that had been found and marked by someone else. As the historian Peter Laslett concludes, 'It is gratuitous to turn Locke's doctrine of property into the classic doctrine of the "spirit of capitalism"' (Laslett 1960: 106–7).

Ferguson, like Locke, did not confine reason or civil society to mercantile capitalism. 'The inhabitants of a village in some primitive age, may have safely been intrusted to the conduct of reason' to regulate their own affairs (Ferguson 1995: 63). The Iroquois Confederacy of the seventeenth and eighteenth centuries was described by the French missionary and anthropologist Joseph-François Lafitau (1681–1746). The Confederacy linked six Native American nations, including the Mohawk and Seneca, who united to defend their rights in the fur trade and block the movement of European settlers into the interior of what is now New York State. Iroquois women cultivated crops, and rights to land were transmitted through women. Men, who hunted and engaged in the fur trade, joined their wives' lineage. Ferguson (1995: 64) concluded that the Confederacy was rationally sustained. We tend to exaggerate the misery of barbarous times, Ferguson comments, because we imagine 'what we ourselves should suffer in a situation to which we are not accustomed' (103). Every age has its consolations. In barbarous times, persons and properties were secure, because everyone had a friend who would protect one, according to maxims of honour and generosity (104).

Evolution as progress?

Auguste Comte (1798–1857), who has sometimes been identified as the founder of sociology, argued that society cannot be reduced to its component individuals. Institutions are like organs in the body of an animal; the function of the part is determined by its place in the whole. This has become known as the 'organic analogy'. Herbert Spencer (1820–1903) developed this analogy during the middle years of the nineteenth century, regarding social progress as the consequence of the evolution of social systems. Spencer considered that societies develop like animal or plant organisms. In contrast to Darwin's theory of natural selection, in which random variations between individuals in a population have different consequences for survival in a particular environment, Spencer's theory postulated an internal dynamic driving populations toward increasing complexity (Spencer 1972 [1857]: 39). Spencer and Comte associated the evolution of society with the evolution of thought, from irrational superstition to rational science. The view became dangerously embedded in early twentieth-century sociology and can be detected in the work of the German sociologist Max Weber (1864–1920), to whom we refer below.

Ferguson differs from Locke, Hobbes and Rousseau in constructing a sequence of stages in the evolution of human society. But they are stages in the evolution of property, from savagery (hunting and gathering) to barbarism (nomadic herding), *not* stages in the evolution of rationality. The only property of a hunter-gatherer is his weapons, utensils and clothing. Because hunting is collective, game once caught belongs to the community, as do the crops that the women plant and harvest collectively in native North America. Nor is that state based on ignorance: 'Men are conscious of their equality, and are tenacious of its rights' (Ferguson 1995: 83).

Ferguson did not see the commercially oriented country in which he lived as the epitome of rationally organised civil society. On the contrary, he was concerned that civil society seemed under threat. Far from tracing the origin of civil society to the eighteenth century, he was worried about its disappearance. 'Ruder' nations tend to succumb to the better-organised armies of more civilised nations, but this does not justify an assumption of superiority (Ferguson 1995: 94). In commercially based societies the national spirit may be neglected because people rely on the agencies of the state to uphold social order. Society thus becomes increasingly divided into separate callings, 'and society is made to consist of parts, of which none is animated with the spirit of society itself . . . Men cease to be good citizens' (Ferguson 1995: 207). The members of a community, like those of a conquered province, lose their sense of kindred or neighbourhood, and have no common affairs to transact except those of trade. 'The mighty engine which we suppose to have formed society, only tends to set its members at variance, or to continue their intercourse after the bonds of affection are broken' (24).

Self-interest and social relationships

Seligman agrees with Ferguson that a commercial economy did not necessarily promote social cohesion (Seligman 1992:

138). It is, however, questionable whether Seligman represents Ferguson correctly when he writes of 'the central and
growing realisation [in the eighteenth century] that man is
motivated by two divergent and contradictory principles –
altruism and egoism' (Seligman 1992: 26). This is a Weberian
proposition (Weber 1947: 116). It is true that Ferguson writes
at times as if it were only our inherent sociability that checks
self-interest. If humans were primarily concerned with their
own subsistence, he argues, we would be reduced to the level
of animals, in which other people were merely useful or detri-
mental. In fact, we value social relationships more highly
than subsistence (Ferguson 1995: 35–6). Elsewhere, however,
Ferguson puts forward the stronger argument that people
enter into social relations out of self-interest. Before the state
assumed responsibility for upholding the law, people owed
their safety to 'the warm attachment of their friends, and to
the exercise of every talent which could render them respected,
feared or beloved' (211). 'Intangled together by the reciprocal ties of dependence and protection, . . . the subjects of
monarchy, like those of republics, find themselves occupied
as members of an active society, and engaged to treat with
their fellow-creatures on a liberal footing' (71). In a more
'rude' state, wealth can be unequally divided, but the differences do not amount to much: 'To enjoy their magnificence
they must live in a croud [*sic*]; and to secure their possessions
they must be surrounded by friends that espouse their quar-
rels' (238). For Ferguson, I believe, the interesting question
was: Why does commercial capitalism undermine the coincidence of self-interest and reciprocal or co-operative social
relations?

There is no basis in the work of Locke and Ferguson
for constructing binary oppositions around the construct
modern = rational, pre-modern = non-rational or 'primordial'.

The restriction of civil society to the modern bourgeoisie was introduced by Adam Smith and Karl Marx (see Gouldner 1980: 356–7, Tester 1992: 49, and Kingston-Mann 2003 on Marx's changing views). The German sociologist Max Weber is best known for arguing that the Protestant doctrine of free will facilitated the rise of capitalism, but he also constructed an influential theory of political organisation in which he contrasted 'traditional' with 'bureaucratic' government. The equation of rational with 'modern' and irrational with 'pre-modern' is based on Weber's theory of development from traditional to bureaucratic government, that is, from blind adherence to tradition, to acceptance of a rational order (Weber 1947: 300, 327). Locke and Ferguson cannot be cited in support of the claim that universal citizenship was developed in the eighteenth and nineteenth centuries to create a broader solidarity to replace that based on 'particular and often *primordial* criteria of trust and solidarity' (Seligman 1992: 146, my emphasis). Seligman, however, repeatedly opposes rational to primordial social relations. Ties between individuals are no longer 'defined by a tradition of *primordial* "givenness" (membership of a territorial or kinship collective)' (Seligman 1992: 69, my emphasis). Seligman attributes recent ethnic nationalism in southeastern Europe to 'particular, *primordial* criteria of membership, trust and solidarity' (151). The case of Yugoslavia, outlined above, shows this is an over-simplification. Bette Denich points out that, at a critical point in the break-up of Yugoslavia, adoption of ethnic identities became a rational strategy. Jobs and housing and therefore, she argues, personal survival depended on how the new state would be constituted and in whose name. 'If the state was to be redefined, average citizens needed to redefine their way of accessing it and had reason to fear being "left out in the cold" in the prospective power allocation along ethnic lines' (Denich 2003: 191). Discovering or reasserting ethnic identity was not an innate or irrational impulse.

Medieval civil society

Both Tester and Seligman claim that in feudal society there was 'no distinction between public and private' (Tester 1992: 14, Seligman 1992: 30–1; Tester attributes this claim to Hegel and Marx). This is simply not true. In the thirteenth century, the village communal assembly already operated effectively in France and Switzerland to co-ordinate peasant resistance against feudal overlords (Bloch 1966: 168–70, Viazzo 1989: 266). In England, the village community was 'in a position voluntarily to accept fresh responsibility, to bind itself to the fulfillment of obligations, and to incur financial liabilities ... [but] its legal status is not easy to define' (Cam 1962: 79). Opposition to feudal lords was usually undertaken by individuals or small groups, although villagers sometimes successfully bargained collectively over the terms of their tenancies (Hilton 1962). The situation in France was quite different. Everyone understood that public matters were resolved by bargaining between rival centres of power: the corporate village on the one hand, and the nobility or king on the other (Mendras and Cole 1991: 127). My own archival research in eastern France (Layton 2000) revealed that the villages of Franche Comté were repeatedly subject to demands for tribute during the later years of the *ancien régime*. Documents stored in the village hall at Pellaport, the locus of my research, recorded that in 1673, for example, Pellaport's assembly challenged the allegation made by monks from a local monastery that they had deliberately defrauded the monastery by mixing oats with the barley paid as a tithe. In 1761, a local seigneur attempted to reactivate feudal rights which, he claimed, had belonged to earlier holders of the seigneurie and were recorded in documents dated 1549 and 1657. Pellaport's village assembly responded that it was an incontestable principle of French law that, to enter into a tributary relationship with a seigneur, two-thirds of the inhabitants must give their consent, at a freely convened meeting. The assembly produced documentary evidence to show that in 1657 there were between thirty and forty households in the village, yet the seigneur's document had only been signed by seven men, some of whom were already bound to the seigneur of the time by other obligations. Similar arguments were used to reject the 1549 contract.

A long-standing school of political thought in England held that the peasant village was the cradle of democracy. This school's views are in the same spirit as Kropotkin's and directly opposed to those of Seligman, Tester and Gellner. The type of community it extolled was typical of the Open Field (Champion) zone, which extended in a broad band from Dorset and Sussex, through the Midlands, to Yorkshire. Between the tenth and eighteenth centuries, each English village under the open field regime chose a jury at its village court. The court admitted new freeholders and tenants to the community, and passed by-laws compelling residents to repair chimneys and clear pathways and forbidding them to encroach on access tracks by over-ploughing the edge of strips or to allow animals to graze on fields before crops had been harvested. The jury also limited the number of animals each household could graze on commons (Ault 1972, Chibnall 1965: 231, Orwin and Orwin 1938: 154–9).

Advocates of village government as the source of democracy traced its origin to Germanic customs brought to England by the Anglo-Saxons. The Victorian historian

Edward Freeman visited Switzerland in 1863, and witnessed a local public assembly. He described the experience as 'the realisation of a dream . . . to see [men] discharge the immemorial rights of Teutonic freemen . . . the eternal democracy . . . the constitution which was of immemorial antiquity in the days of Tacitus' (quoted in Burrow 1981: 169). In the seventeenth century the Anglo-Saxon origins of English society were used to develop the theory of the 'Norman yoke'. According to this theory the English had lived before 1066 as free and equal citizens, governing themselves through representative institutions brought to England by Anglo-Saxon settlers (Hill 1958: 64). While it disregarded the fact that there was already social inequality in Anglo-Saxon England, the historian Christopher Hill suggests the idea had probably been current throughout the Middle Ages (compare MacDougall 1982: 57). Supporters of parliament argued that English common law stemmed from Anglo-Saxon times and had survived the conquest, providing a legal precedent for the principle that the king was answerable to the people. For the Levellers, a radical political sect active during the English Civil War who campaigned against the monarchy and private property, the Germanic village community realised the natural rights of man (Hill 1958: 81). Ferguson may have had this tradition in mind when he referred to self-governing villages in 'some primitive age'.

Hill (1958: 76) accepts the broad thrust of the historical argument, claiming that early Anglo-Saxon society was certainly much freer than the Norman society that supplanted it. The difficulty, he notes, was that little was known about the actual form of Anglo-Saxon society (and, one might add, even less about the earlier society described by Tacitus; see Layton 2003: 106–7). The essential weakness of the historical school of thought was that it failed to explain why the supposed Germanic customs had survived, to show whose interests they served and to explain how such people had been able to perpetuate them. It fails, as Hill wrote, to see 'society as a whole, with institutions and ideas themselves related to the social structure, and of relative not absolute validity' (Hill 1958: 116).

The enclosures – two visions of civil society

The village democracy celebrated by writers such as Freeman came to an end with the enclosures. Enclosure privatised common land and dissolved the communal village institutions that had managed common resources. Enclosure impacted most heavily on the Open Field zone. The open field system originated in later Anglo-Saxon times as a way of managing an economy based on both cereal cultivation and livestock rearing. The better land near the village was divided into individually owned strips of land that was ploughed and on which cereals were grown. The strips were long and narrow to accommodate the difficulty of turning heavy, medieval wheeled ploughs pulled by oxen; the more oblong the strip, the fewer the number of times the plough had to be turned at each end. Households' strips were intermixed to ensure each family had access to different types of soil. A long, narrow strip has, however, a much greater perimeter than a square field of the same area. Keeping livestock away from the cereal fields precluded the need to fence the land. Livestock were herded on the poorer land farther from the village. Keeping the village livestock together allowed one person to look after many more animals than a single household would have owned, freeing others to work in the fields. In order to rest and reinvigorate the plough land, strips were grouped into larger 'open fields', one of which was left fallow in any year. Livestock also grazed on the fallow, manuring the soil.

The open field system was thus a very effective adaptation to medieval agriculture. It was displaced for a number of reasons. Some households began to plant crops formerly confined to gardens, such as peas and beans, on the fallow. Legumes also rejuvenate the soil, but must be fenced against livestock. Innovative households came to see the strict collective regulation of the open field system as old fashioned. A number of recent authors have, however, argued that the principal drive to abolish the open fields came from large landlords who wanted to develop new crops, to take advantage of the growing market in agriculture. Smallholders had to be turned into tenants and the commons brought under cultivation.

The political arguments for and against enclosure reveal the emergence of two schools of thought that persist in the modern debate concerning civil society. Promoters of enclosure would support the claim that civil society 'can be said to equal the milieu of private contractual relations' (Tester 1992: 8). Its opponents would advocate the claim that civil society is 'a web of autonomous associations . . . which bind citizens together in matters of common concern' (Tester 1992: 8, citing Charles Taylor). Claims that commons were overstocked and that grazing was unstinted (i.e. unregulated) were used to justify enclosure (Neeson 1993: 36–7), but there are many documented examples of village juries enforcing control of common land through fines (Neeson 1993: 88, 116).

Since the 1970s there has been renewed debate about the effective management of common land. The political scientist Garrett Hardin (1968), reviving the ideas of William Lloyd (Lloyd 1964 [1833]), held that, unless coercion is applied by an authority, common property is inevitably less well managed than private property. If there are no controls over access, self-restraint by some households in the number of animals they graze will be undermined when others put too many animals on the commons. These free-riders cause degradation of the niche on which all depend, but they are the only ones to benefit from the higher numbers of stock they have pastured. The rational strategy is therefore for everyone to overstock, destroying the commons' value. Hardin argued that only sanctions imposed by government, or privatising the commons, would enable responsible management. He discounted the possibility of self-regulation among the users.

The other school, founded by the political scientists and anthropologist Bonnie McCay and James Acheson (1987) and Elinor Ostrom (1990), uses aspects of neo-Darwinian theory to argue that individual and collective ownership are both adaptive, but to different circumstances. Self-regulation depends on limiting access to, and use of, a shared resource. The commons must therefore be treated as a territory.

Socio-ecology studies social behaviour according to the principles of Darwinian evolution. It differs from the more determinist approaches of sociobiology and evolutionary psychology in allowing learned, cultural behaviour an important role in human social evolution, but argues that where several alternative social strategies are practised, the strategy that offers the best adaptation to the local social and natural environment will tend to replace competing ones. The socio-ecological theory of territoriality was originally developed to explain animal behaviour, and first applied to human territoriality by Rada Dyson-Hudson and Eric Alden Smith (Dyson-Hudson and Smith 1978). The theory holds that it will only be adaptive to defend the boundaries of a territory if the resources within it are sufficiently dense and predictable to outweigh the costs of defence. When resources are scarce and unpredictable, it is a waste of effort for individual households to fence off small portions because the risk of resources within each patch failing will be too great to justify their defence. Dyson-Hudson and Smith argued that the cattle-herding Karimojong of East Africa defend grazing land as a 'tribe' because the distribution of grass and water is too unpredictable to justify dividing it into small areas defended by individual lineages. Small fields of maize are, on the other hand, defended by the Karimojong households who cultivate them. The geographer Robert Netting used the same argument in his analysis of land ownership in the Swiss village of Törbel. Grass on the alpine pastures is too dispersed and unreliable to justify the cost and risk of dividing it into fields owned by individual households. Collective management is more efficient. Privately owned fields are located on lower, richer soils (Netting 1981: 60–7).

Far from allowing open access to the commons in Törbel, use of the alpine commons is closely regulated by the community. Only citizens of the village are allowed to use it and the number of cattle they can graze is controlled. McCay and Acheson point out that, under the medieval and post-medieval open field system, use of English commons was also generally regulated by the communities to which they belonged. Ostrom argues that Hardin's model is not wrong, but lacks the generality Hardin claimed for it. The 'open-access' scenario proposed by Hardin is not the only possibility. The application of game theory to the study of the evolution of social strategies predicts the conditions in which individuals can form stable coalitions based on mutual trust that can avert the 'tragedy' of over-exploitation. When individuals interact repeatedly co-operation can become a stable strategy (see discussion of the 'Prisoner's Dilemma' in chapter 2). People who interact regularly in a local context, who have developed shared norms and patterns of reciprocity, who can monitor whether their associates are adhering to the agreed level of exploitation and who can punish free-riders are most likely to succeed (Ostrom 1990: 184–8). Intense pressure to conform develops in fire crews, army units etc. as well as in peasant villages. The historian J. M. Neeson claims overstocking on English common land was rare and that deliberate overstocking was in fact a strategy used by wealthy landowners who advocated enclosure, to justify their argument that common grazing was inefficient (Neeson 1993: 88, 116). McCay and Acheson argue, in opposition to Hardin and Lloyd, that the English enclosures were precipitated by conditions peculiar to the rise of capitalism (improvements in agricultural methods and the growth of a market for farm products) and not by an inherent weakness in commons management.

Gouldner traces the origin of civil society to the 'independent self-managed social organisation outside of the feudal structure that developed in the West both in villages and towns' (Gouldner 1980: 361) and opponents of enclosure condemned the loss of village democracy (e.g. Nourse, quoted in Neeson 1993: 20). They argued that destroying village society through enclosure also endangered relations in the nation as a whole, bringing about an open dissatisfaction that risked mob rule (Neeson 1993: 22).

Supporters of enclosure argued that common property was a more primitive condition than private property; fenmen in East Anglia were compared to Native Americans and Tartars (Neeson 1993: 30–1). Here one can detect the origin of Seligman and Gellner's treatment of 'primordial ties' (for the wider currency of this idea, see Duffield 2001: 110). European 'progressives' saw private property as the source of all virtue, from economic initiatives to high moral character: in *The wealth of nations* Adam Smith linked the advance of reason to private property; Blackstone's *Commentaries* links private property, and the right to exclude others, to freedom (Kingston-Mann 1999: 10–20). Accounts of the English agricultural revolution published by Toynbee and Prothero in the 1880s captured popular imagination by attributing particular innovations to 'great men' who triumphed over a conservative mass of country bumpkins (Overton 1996: 3). All these claims are antecedents of the approach taken by Seligman and Gellner.

Whether enclosure was really necessary to implement improvements in agriculture is debated. Agricultural development originated among smallholders in the Netherlands and took place without enclosure in parts of France and Germany (see Layton 2000: 84–6, 261, 336–46). Michael Havinden (1961) wrote that, although it is customary to regard open field agriculture as backward and static, many of the most important advances in open field farming in Oxfordshire were made before the idea of agricultural progress became popular in the eighteenth century (cf. Neeson 1993: 157). Arthur Young ignored his own discovery that the same outmoded techniques were used on both open and enclosed fields, and that enclosure had little effect on yields (Kingston-Mann 1999: 17–18). Mark Overton (1996) similarly questions the view that technological innovations in English agriculture were facilitated by enclosures; small farmers accomplished much growth in productivity in the seventeenth century, and the eighteenth-century revolution was one of landlords appropriating income from farming (Overton 1996: 6–7, citing Allen 1991). As techniques improved and the market for crops grew, enclosed land came to be worth more, probably 30 per cent more, than open field land. This attracted owners who intended to rent land to tenants. Abolition of tithes at enclosure increased the profits owners could make (Overton 1996: 163).

Enclosure did not bring greater democracy to rural communities. During the time between the abolition of village juries and the Local Government Act of 1894, unelected Justices of the Peace – often the local squires – were responsible for local government (Newby et al. 1978: 221–4, Plumb 1990: 34–5, Wilson and Game 1994: 42). Seligman (1992: 105) points out that the first English Reform Bill of 1832 left five out of six men disenfranchised. Even the reforms of 1884–5 excluded about half the urban male working class from citizenship. Civil society was under threat. And, as Marx insisted, wage labour is another form of disenfranchisement.

The view advocated by Gellner and Seligman, that civil society is uniquely associated with private property and a commercial economy, was thus born in a contest over who would own and manage English farmland. Seligman reproduces the enclosers' view when he claims that feudalism lacked the complete realisation of 'a civil society of autonomous, moral, and economic individual agents' (Seligman 1992: 107). The civil society of the open field village stood in the way of powerful interests. Dissolving that society released the land it controlled. Rural riots against enclosure were disciplined events aimed at preserving common rights and face-to-face marketing (Overton 1996: 190). Ester Kingston-Mann notes that Marxist opposition to the Russian village community, the *mir*, was also based on the threat semi-autonomous communities posed to the power of the state. 'Soviet officials viewed the localism and autonomy of the commune as a danger to the state's monopolistic claims to leadership, authority and control' (Kingston-Mann 1999: 183). Marxists turned their attention to the urban proletariat because they found it difficult 'to establish their social control over a social element which still possessed powerful ties to family, land and community' (175).

The debate has continued. The claim that the open field system prevented rational land management can be compared to T. E. Day's description of Aboriginal land in central Australia as 'dormant wealth lying about in almost criminal uselessness' (Day 1916, quoted in Layton 1986: 64). According to Day, only cattle ranching, and the consequent fencing of the land, would realise that wealth. John Cowper's comment in 1732, that 'the profit of a few landlords was nothing compared to the "Good of the Whole"' (Neeson 1993: 21) parallels that of a missionary who objected to pastoral settlement of central Australia. 'This great area the source of food to such a considerable number of natives may not be taken from them for the benefit of one white man' (Albrecht 1937, quoted in Layton 1986: 65). The archaeologist Randall McGuire describes two common reactions among white Americans to the traditional Pueblo society of the native southwest. Collier was a Superintendent of Indian Affairs who advocated Indian self-government in the southwest, but 'where Collier and his reformers had found communal co-operation, the conservatives [who sought to abolish native land tenure] found the violation of individual rights and freedoms' (McGuire 2002: 139). The analytical waters become muddied when the proponents of a social order that may well be appropriate in particular circumstances elevate that strategy to a political ideology for which they claim universal validity.

CONCLUSION

At the start of this chapter three questions were posed:

- How should 'civil society' be defined?
- Is civil society necessarily associated with a commercial economy or can it occur under different regimes?
- Does civil society necessarily tend to support or undermine the state?

I have argued that, to avoid prejudice, a descriptive definition is necessary, defining civil society as 'the social structures occupying the space between the household and the state that enable people to co-ordinate their management of resources and activities'. Much of the recent discussion of civil society concerns the engagement between civil organisations and the state. To appreciate how such engagement occurs, however, we need to look at a broader field of organisations and investigate the circumstances that bring about their political mobilisation at particular times. A functional definition that specifies what role civil society should play in relation to the state (whether it should oppose or uphold state policy) will inevitably be qualified by the writer's evaluation of the state. The claim that civil society, and the rational human social behaviour that underpins it, is uniquely associated with commercial capitalism originated in the enclosure debate and is too politically biased to underpin the cross-cultural study of civil society. Seligman concedes, 'I am not arguing here that the existence of group identities as such militates against the existence of civil society' (Seligman 1992: 163). Voluntary associations, political parties, interest and corporate groups are, he admits, vital. But groups of this kind, Seligman contends, are different to ethnic groups. Only the former are organised 'for the pursuit of mutual interest on the institutional level' (164). However, this is precisely the purpose of ethnic nationalist associations. According to Seligman, only ethnic groups 'posit an alternative moral vision to that of society at large' (164), but political parties do just that! Seligman claims that only voluntary associations, corporate groups etc. are based on 'instrumental-rational modes of behaviour'. But in a zero-sum game, as in post-communist Yugoslavia, ethnic exclusionism may be very 'rational'. If the concept of civil society was devised to explain how people acting rationally in their self-interest can create a stable fabric of social relations (as Locke and Ferguson argued), this approach should be tested against all forms of human society, seeking to establish which forms of society most effectively promote self-interest in different social and natural environments.

Self-interest and social evolution

CIVIL SOCIETY IN LOCKE'S STATE OF NATURE

The individual and society

Chapter 2 reconsiders the question posed by Adam Ferguson: is there a contest between commitment to social relationships and selfishness, or is it in the individual's interest to sustain social relationships? The chapter gives some examples that show how people strive for order as much as for disorder. It argues that success or failure in sustaining social relations must be explained by the 'ecology' of social interaction. What are the benefits to the individual of investing in social relationships? Different social strategies are most likely to succeed in different social environments and, if the social context deteriorates (as it did with the collapse of socialism in Yugoslavia), people may respond by narrowing the scope of their social relationships. The chapter therefore also asks to what extent ecological approaches to biological evolution can provide appropriate models for explaining social process. Chapter 3 will use this framework as a basis for analysing the breakdown of social order.

Thomas Hobbes envisaged the natural human condition as one of random disorder, in which every individual sought their self-preservation by trying to control others (Hobbes 1970: 65). People would only be willing to work for the general good if they could be confident anyone who cheated was punished. Just as Garrett Hardin supposed 'freedom in a commons brings ruin for all' through over-exploitation (Hardin 1968: 1244), so Hobbes imagined that people living in the 'natural human condition' would readily surrender sufficient personal freedom to a chosen sovereign to enable him to enforce peace. Chapter 1 recalled that John Locke disagreed with Hobbes's claim that the natural human condition was a war of every man against every other man. Locke argued that people could live together according to reason, without a sovereign, an insight that anthropology and behavioural ecology have confirmed (not least through showing that co-operative management of common property can be sustainable). Locke agreed, however, that men living together without a higher authority are vulnerable to the state of war because there is no one authorised to intervene (see chapter 1). Hobbes's main aim was to construct a logical opposition between order and disorder, rather than to identify an actual condition against which contemporary European society could be assessed (Hill 1958: 271). Even if his answer seems simplistic, Hobbes identified an important problem that Locke acknowledged, and people are still attempting to answer: how can people create a condition in which it is to their advantage to forgo individual, *immediate* selfish goals in order that they themselves may benefit in the long run? Recent research has converged with, or returned to, Hobbes's dilemma, but provided more detailed answers that explain the relationship between social order and anarchy. On the one hand authors such as Napoleon Chagnon (whom we will assess in chapter 4) argue that endemic warfare is indeed characteristic of small-scale societies; on the other hand behavioural ecologists (socio-ecologists) follow Locke in arguing that co-operation and reciprocity can develop through natural selection or rational self-interest. Most importantly, behavioural ecologists have shown why social order does not always depend on a sovereign. Locke was right to argue that the 'state of nature' was not necessarily a war of every man against every other man. The first part of this chapter looks at the ways in which social order can be sustained in self-governing, local communities. The second part adopts an evolutionary perspective, in order to assess the conditions that make social strategies sustainable or unsustainable.

Social scientists have long been suspicious of evolutionary theory, both because it focuses on hereditary traits and because it takes the individual as the unit of analysis. This chapter will argue, against such suspicion, that there is scope for a fruitful reconciliation between evolutionary and social theory. The debate originates partly in the work of the sociologists Herbert Spencer (1820–1903) and Emile Durkheim (1858–1917), who argued that the good of society took precedence over the good of its individual members and that society therefore upheld laws for its own benefit. Spencer and Durkheim were right to recognise that society is an 'emergent' phenomenon. Language, law, kinship, government are created by social interaction and are not properties of the solitary individual. Chapters 3 and 4 will return to this insight. Human evolution has taken place for millions of years in a social environment, and the individual has become adapted to benefit from the advantages of living in society. However Durkheim (1938 [1901]) went further, arguing that when the individual fulfils family obligations, when he worships at a church or accepts contract law, he is conforming to social phenomena that impose themselves on him regardless of his individual will. While conforming to the requirements of society the individual may not be aware of its constraints. Once he steps out of line, Durkheim argued, society enforces its morality through public ridicule and its laws by formal punishment, either as repression or as restitution. Many social scientists therefore consider it inappropriate to take the individual as the unit of analysis when studying social life.

There is an interesting coincidence between the development of this theory and the rise of the European nation state, which is hinted at in the work of the French postmodernist philosopher Michel Foucault. Durkheim may have unwittingly incorporated statist ideology into his theory. Foucault (1977) challenged the prevailing view that the Enlightenment brought in a new respect for the rights of the individual as citizen. Foucault associates the Enlightenment with the transition of methods of social control from the public display of punishment to more insidious means, from torture to discipline. Surveillance and discipline are, he argues, tools of the modern state first developed in the Prussian army to straighten those who deviate from the 'common good'. Concealed, or justified in terms of the collective good, such practices in fact (Foucault argued) benefit a powerful elite. Isaiah Berlin (Berlin 2002: 47, 68) similarly regarded the equation of the individual will with that of the state, and the idea that an elite is uniquely qualified to govern, as the two principal enemies of individual freedom.

A Darwinian evolutionary approach starts from the opposite extreme to Durkheim by asking how upholding conventional rules may work to the *individual's* advantage rather than the group's. This offers a way of moving beyond Durkheim's collectivist approach. Anthropologists tend to address this type of question by looking at the simplest human societies, where the fundamental aspects of social life can most clearly be seen. Useful though it is as a starting point, the analysis of reciprocity and co-operation among hunter-gatherers evades the issues of power identified by Foucault that need to be addressed once analysis moves to more complex societies.

Some aspects of the Functionalist school, which dominated anthropology in Britain from the 1920s to the 1950s and was paralleled in the work of the US sociologist Talcott Parsons, are consistent with evolutionary theory, but other aspects follow in Durkheim's footsteps. The anthropologist Bronislaw Malinowski proposed a theory of social behaviour consistent with Darwinian evolutionary theory. He defined the function of a custom as 'satisfying (the individual's) primary biological needs through the instrumentalities of culture' (Malinowski 1954: 202). Malinowski carried out extensive fieldwork on the Trobriand Islands of the western Pacific. A complex network of trading relations between islands was sustained by alliances between leading men who exchanged valuable shell armbands and necklaces as tokens of their continuing relationship. Malinowski saw the Trobriand islander of the Pacific as a reasonable man, manipulating the possibilities in social relations to his advantage, although unaware of the total network of relations to which he contributed. Malinowski's islander is very similar to John Locke's rational participant in civil society.

The dominant school of functionalism led by Alfred Radcliffe-Brown followed Durkheim in subsuming the interests of individuals to the interests of 'the social system' and thus perpetuating the split between social and biological scientists. The behaviour of individuals provides examples of customs, but to be truly scientific, Radcliffe-Brown argued, the anthropologist should build up a picture of regularities in the emergent social order. His aim was to discover how institutions 'work together with a sufficient degree of harmony or internal consistency [to continue as a system], i.e. without producing persistent conflicts which can neither be resolved or regulated' (Radcliffe-Brown 1952: 181). Radcliffe-Brown's approach risks committing the 'group selection' fallacy, of assuming individuals who suppress their self-interest in favour of the common good will prosper at the expense of the selfish. The difficulty with this hypothesis is that, if such social behaviour were for example genetically determined, those individuals who forgo their own selfish reproductive interests to benefit others will not transmit their altruistic genes to the next generation. On the contrary, altruism will be displaced by selfishness and, by analogy, the same outcome will apply where people act through rational self-interest: the selfish will flourish at the expense of those who sacrifice their own interests to benefit 'society' or 'the group' (see Trivers 1985: 79–85). The 'Tragedy of the Commons' is a famous example of this difficulty that arises where it is impossible to control the use of a scarce communal resource. If some people cannot be prevented from over-exploiting the resource, then others will not benefit from showing restraint: their restraint merely leaves more for the 'free-riders' to take beyond their fair share. Garrett Hardin (1968) predicted that once over-exploitation of a common resource begins, everyone will therefore abandon restraint and grab as much as they can of the diminishing resource before it disappears. This is a genuine risk, but Hardin was wrong to argue that it was inevitable, since there are numerous historical examples of common resources that have been successfully managed by local communities. Hence, too, the logical problem that Adam Ferguson identified in his history of civil society: are the principles of altruism and egoism contradictory, or can people advance their self-interest by contributing to social relationships? In order to explore this problem, I shall therefore start with some examples from small-scale communities but then consider stability at the level of the nation state.

Two examples

When confronted with the evidence for violence in small-scale and frontier societies (e.g. Wrangham and Peterson 1996: 77), it is easy to overlook the fact that people are also striving to limit violence and create order. The first two case studies are therefore taken from the Inuit and the nineteenth-century South African colonial frontier. The Inuit present an interesting paradox: they had one of the simplest social systems known among recent human societies yet, among hunter-gatherers, they had one of the most complex technologies, which they needed to survive in the Arctic. There were only two essential roles in traditional Inuit society, those of adult man and adult woman (I am here glossing over the cultural importance of the shaman). The nuclear family formed the basic social unit. Husband and wife were absolutely dependent on one another for survival. But the nuclear family is not isolated. Between 300 and 600 people belonged to a 'community' which owned a territory, and there was a high degree of co-operation between families in the same community. Each community was called 'the people of' (-miut) their territory (Nunamiut, Taremiut), and its members combined to defend the territory and its resources against outsiders.

Successful Inuit hunters gained respect, and might attract followers, becoming leaders in their community, but leadership in traditional Inuit society was based on consensus, not power. There was no guarantee a man would succeed to his father's status, nor that a man's sons would inherit his property. The Inuit lived in a risky environment, and were willing to share belongings because everyone knew relative status could easily be reversed. 'The most fundamental consideration in traditional Northwestern Alaskan strategies of affiliation was that not a single goal in life, including the basic one of sheer survival, could be achieved without the help of kinsmen' (Burch 1975: 198).

There were few rules of social conduct that merited punishment if they were broken. The essential principle was that

the active adults on whom everyone else depended had to survive. The two basic offences were therefore stealing a married
woman and killing a hunter. If either of these offences was
committed, the community expected the wronged husband,
or the dead man's relatives, to gain redress through 'self-help'.
Wife-stealing within the community was dealt with through
the song-duel, in which the man who best entertained the
audience with the ridicule he directed at his rival had the right
to keep the woman. It was more difficult to deal with a case
of murder. The expected response was to kill the murderer,
but one man's revenge is another's murder, and a chain of
retaliatory killings could descend into a feud that threatened
everyone.

E. Adamson Hoebel argued the difference between a murderer who only killed one person and one who killed many was
that the first committed a private offence against the dead man's
family, but the second committed a public offence against the
whole community. Killing several hunters threatened everyone's food supply. Both offences were judged at what Hoebel
called 'the bar of public opinion'. The response was, however, different. 'A single murder is a *private wrong* redressed
by the kinsmen of the victim . . . Repeated murder becomes
a *public crime* punishable by death at the hands of the agent
of the community' (Hoebel 1954: 88). It was vital that the
executioner first obtained community approval. Hoebel cites
a case (described by Boas 1888: 668) in which the headman
of the Akudmirmiut gained permission to execute a multiple
murderer: 'When such approval is obtained no blood revenge
may be taken on the executioner for his act is not murder.
It is the execution of a public [offender]' (Hoebel 1954: 88;
cf. Burch 1975: 198, 204, and Mary-Rousselière 1984: 440–1).

Black frontiers (Kemp 1932) is a vivid first-hand account of
the Johannesburg gold rush of 1886 that graphically conveys

the lack of social order among gold miners on the colonial frontier. Sam Kemp left England at the age of seventeen, and sailed to Durban, trekking from Durban to Pretoria. While he was in Pretoria, news spread that gold had been found thirty-six miles away. There was a wild stampede to the gold fields, and the town of Johannesburg sprang up, a single straggling main street. Kemp describes the scene as follows:

Eastward of the spot where the town mushroomed into existence was an outcropping, a reef of greyish rock. In the sand around it and extending yards on both sides was gold, plenty of gold . . .

Obviously the first problem was to stake out a claim along the reef. That was easy enough, but a far more difficult task was holding that claim against all comers. Somewhere in the seething settlement a mining commissioner was supposed to be located, but no one seemed to know who he was or where he kept himself hidden. The result was a grand jamboree, a free-for-all. Gun-play started very soon; it grew wilder during the days that followed.

The state had evidently abdicated its sovereignty. Social order was at its most tenuous; narrow self-interest held sway until, eventually, a spate of murders led 'the more respectable – or more timid citizens' to propose the appointment of a marshal, supported by a judge and public prosecutor. No one wanted to take on any of the posts. It was, as Kemp puts it, 'a suicide club'. Eventually a seemingly meek Englishman nicknamed Lispy Jones accepted the job of marshal, but the murders continued. 'Every criminal had a group of friends who would lie themselves black in the face, or, if necessary, make things extremely disagreeable for the judge, prosecutor and jury.' Kemp reluctantly agreed to become Lispy Jones's deputy. Matters reached a head after an eight-man gang of strangers raided one of the bars and stole all the gold from thirty or forty gamblers. No one dared shoot until the gang left the bar, then someone belatedly shot out the lights and the gang escaped to 'a blind canyon twenty miles from town'. For once the town was united against a common enemy. Lispy Jones assembled a posse, choosing eight of the best shots in town. On arrival at the canyon he told his party to wait, as the bandits were trapped. Hargreaves, the gang's hardened leader, came out and challenged Lispy to a duel. To avoid unnecessary bloodshed, Jones accepted. The two men rode toward each other, firing their revolvers. Miraculously, Lispy triumphed. Their leader dead, the entire gang surrendered as agreed, and were taken back to Johannesburg. 'Without friends to perjure themselves or help shoot their way out, the criminals were convicted and sentenced to death.' Evidently Hargreaves made two mistakes. The first was to steal gold from so many people at once that his gang, like the Inuit multiple murderer, was identified as a threat to the community at large. This error was reinforced by the fact Hargreaves's gang were strangers without local support (Kemp 1932: 23–31). Unfortunately Lispy did not last long and Kemp does not say whether anyone came forward to take his place.

BIOLOGICAL THEORY AND SOCIAL STRATEGIES

Kinship and social adaptations

Kinship and ethnicity provide powerful bases for social groupings within civil society that may undermine the state. Rather than dismissing them as 'primordial' and, by implication, irrational, as did Ernest Gellner and Adam Seligman, they can be better understood by considering what advantages kinship and ethnicity may offer the individual during social life. The most elementary forms of social life among non-human species arise where individual organisms increase their own reproductive fitness by *inter*acting with other members of their own species (Trivers 1985: 41–65). Recognition of kinship is fundamental to interaction in human society (the importance of kinship among the Nuer and Somali was mentioned in chapter 1). The great advantage of kinship as a means of organising social relationships is that it has the potential to shape interaction automatically, from birth. A person is a child of their mother and father, a sibling to their brothers and sisters, and so forth. If membership of a social group is assigned by patrilineal or matrilineal descent, then the person automatically becomes a member of their father's or mother's group. The organisation of social relationships that provide co-operation and reciprocity seems to unroll almost without human intervention, and society to be reproduced of its own accord. Even in our own society, where kinship is relatively unimportant, we commonly know the names of relatives up to the level of second cousin.[1]

There are also good biological reasons why people should prefer to maintain relationships with their kin, rather than strangers. Biological and social scientists have thus investigated the importance of kinship from different angles. Darwinian biological evolution is about success in transmitting genes. Two evolutionary theories to account for the significance of kinship in human social behaviour have been put forward by William Hamilton and Robert Trivers. William Hamilton (1964) developed the first theory to explain how social interaction can contribute to an animal's reproductive success. Hamilton is famous in biology not only for having demonstrated, with mathematical precision, how genetically determined altruistic behaviour toward kin can be favoured through natural selection, but for having his PhD thesis on

---

[1] In a practical conducted with 149 first year anthropology students between 2002 and 2004, 51 per cent could name a great-grandparent and 49 per cent a second cousin, but fewer than 5 per cent a more distant relative.

the subject rejected by examiners – who failed to appreciate its significance – as substandard (Trivers 1985: 47). In
response, Hamilton published two linked papers (Hamilton
1964) that revealed the originality of his ideas. Hamilton's
predictions have been supported by subsequent research that
shows some animal species have evolved fine-tuned abilities
to recognise their relatedness to other individuals and modify
their behaviour accordingly (Trivers 1985: 129–35).

Assuming that social behaviour was entirely under genetic
control, Hamilton asked two questions:

- Under what conditions may it be advantageous, in evolutionary terms, for animals to co-operate with other members of the same species, or to forgo resources to benefit
  another?
- What genetic mechanisms favour the spread of such
  behaviour through natural selection?

In the narrow sense, each individual is competing with every
other one for reproductive success, that is, the successful production of children who will grow up carrying the same genes
as the parent, and in turn transmit these genes to grandchil-
dren. However, the individual does not share genes only with
their parents and children. Genes are also shared with brothers
and sisters, uncles and aunts, first cousins and second cousins.
But the *proportion* of genes held in common decreases with
genealogical distance. The evolutionary biologist Hamilton
argued that if we were more willing to help (even to die for) our
close relatives than our more distant ones, the gene responsible
for such behaviour could increase in frequency over successive generations. 'A gene may receive positive selection even
though disadvantageous to its bearers if it causes them to confer sufficiently large advantages on relatives' (Hamilton 1964:
17). This is called 'kin-selected altruism', and explains why

worker ants and bees have evolved to give their lives to save
the rest of the hive from attack. In a bee or ant nest, all the
workers are children of the same queen. If, therefore, a few
sacrifice their lives to save the colony, the survivors are likely to
carry the same 'altruistic' gene, or gene complex, and transmit
it to successive generations. This extension of the concept of
reproductive success is known as 'inclusive fitness': sacrificing
one's life for the colony does not increase one's personal fitness, but it does ensure one's genes are transmitted to the next
generation. Hamilton predicted that second cousins would lie
at the limit of kin-selected altruism: beyond that, the percent-
age of genes shared between the altruist and the beneficiary
would be too low to justify risking death.

In some cases, Hamilton's theory fits well with human social
behaviour. The Sarakatsani shepherds of northern Greece
behaved as his theory predicts, by refusing to behave altru-
istically to anyone more distant than a second cousin. John
Campbell (Campbell 1964) found that every individual recognised kin on his mother's and father's side to the level of second
cousins. For any individual, the total Sarakatsani community
was divided into two categories: those who were kin, and
those who were strangers (relatives by marriage formed a
third, intermediate category). Confidence, trust and a genuine concern for the other's welfare only existed between
kin. Campbell calculated that an individual's kindred would
contain about 250 people, about half of whom were second
cousins.

As a way of talking about social relations, however,
human 'kinship' often extends beyond biological relatedness
to include adopted children and close friends of one's parents (as fictive 'aunts' and 'uncles'). Hamilton's theory cannot
therefore provide the whole answer. In small-scale societies,
social kinship (that is, the cultural interpretation of biological

relatedness) locates people from birth into social relationships that allow them to call in specific ways upon each other's labour or resources during subsistence activities. Small-scale societies frequently have devices for extending kinship beyond biological relatedness. The hunter-gatherers of the Kalahari have a limited number of personal names. Anyone sharing the same name (a 'namesake') is treated as a brother or sister (Marshall 1957). In Aboriginal Australia, strangers such as white anthropologists or community workers must be assimilated into the local kinship system in order to acquire a social identity. Once integrated, the stranger must avoid all women classed as 'mother-in-law', support his 'brothers' in disputes, respond generously to requests for gifts from his 'brothers-in-law' (to whom he is notionally in debt for a potential wife) and so forth.

The anthropologist Marshall Sahlins (1976) criticised sociobiology's use of kin selection to explain human social behaviour. He pointed out that behaviour toward socially recognised kin often varies independently of the degree of biological relatedness. A very good example of this phenomenon can be seen in the custom known as cross-cousin marriage. Cross cousins are the children of a brother and a sister; children of two brothers or two sisters are referred to as parallel cousins, because the gender of the linking parents is the same. Cross-cousin marriage is practised by a number of small-scale societies in Australia, Southeast Asia and North and South America. Suppose that, in a society where group membership is traced through men (patrilineal descent), and women have to leave their group at marriage, two men in different groups form an alliance by exchanging their sisters in marriage. If the alliance is to be sustained in future generations, cross cousins (mother's brother's children and/or father's sister's children) are ideal marriage partners because they are born into the

A new alliance...

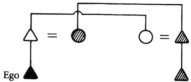

Ego

Whom should ego marry to maintain the alliance?

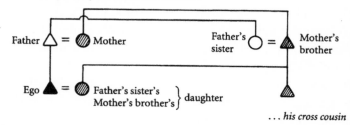

Father = Mother   Father's sister = Mother's brother

Ego = Father's sister's } daughter
      Mother's brother's

... *his cross cousin*

Where are ego's parallel cousins?

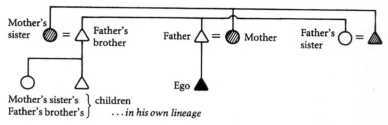

Mother's sister = Father's brother   Father = Mother   Father's sister =

Mother's sister's } children
Father's brother's   ... *in his own lineage*

Ego

Figure 2.1 Development of a Yanomamö marriage alliance.

allied lineage, whereas parallel cousins are born into one's own lineage (Figure 2.1). Parallel cousins are therefore classed as brother and sister, while genetically equally close cross cousins are classed as brother/sister-in-law or wife/husband.

The flexibility of social kinship has also enabled human societies to adjust their behaviour toward kin in ways appropriate to the subsistence economy. Most recent hunter-gatherer societies live in marginal environments where freedom of movement is essential. In order to sustain far-flung social networks the majority of hunter-gatherer societies therefore make no distinction between kin on the mother's and father's side living elsewhere in the region and have equal visiting rights with both. Among nomadic pastoralists, on the other hand, men must co-operate to defend livestock against raids, and the majority of pastoral societies practise patrilineal descent. Rights to cattle are shared by male relatives and a man's rights are inherited by his sons. Among horticulturalists such as the Iroquois (chapter 1) much of the work is done by women, and mother–daughter co-operation has been argued to explain the relatively high incidence of matrilineal descent in such societies. A woman's rights to land are inherited by her daughters (Goldschmidt 1979, Holden and Mace 2003). Where descent is patrilineal women join their husband's group; where descent is matrilineal men join their wife's group.

SOCIAL EVOLUTION AND GAME THEORY

The theoretical background

The flexibility of human social behaviour toward kin demands a theory to explain why different strategies are adopted in different contexts. Social anthropologists long regarded this variability within a single human species as a trump card in their arguments against genetic determinism of the kind implied by Hamilton. Game theory has provided a useful way forward in the reintegration of social and biological theory. Game theory provides explanatory models that are vital to appreciating the relationship between order and anarchy, showing why people work hard to construct social relationships in certain contexts, yet repudiate them if conditions change. The modern theory for the evolution of co-operation originated in John von Neumann and Oskar Morgenstern's *Theory of*

games (1944), a treatise on economics. Morgenstern considered
that economic theory treated economic actors as autonomous
decision-makers. It failed to take proper account of the fact
that economic actors are dependent on one another's decisions;
that they operate in a social milieu (Nasar 1998: 84). Treating
economic negotiations as a game between two players would
help overcome this weakness. Such a micro-approach seems
well suited to the analysis of small-scale social interaction in
local communities but it has also been applied to international
relations (cf. Locke 1960: 98–9). According to Sylvia Nasar,
Morgenstern persuaded von Neumann to set out a mathematical framework for the study of games. The best-developed
part of the theory concerned 'zero-sum two-person games'. In
a zero-sum game the winnings are fixed, and the two players
are therefore in competition to see who can gain the largest
share. Hargreaves and Lispy Jones were playing a zero-sum
game; one's survival would be secured at the cost of the other's
death. When they were proposed, such games of total conflict
did not seem particularly relevant to the social sciences, but
the model was taken up by post-war military strategists. Air
battles were represented as duels between a pair of opposing
planes. There was a trade-off between two conflicting plans:
waiting until the opponent approached, so as to have a better
chance of hitting him, and firing first to avoid being hit. Kemp
describes how 'Lispy spurred forward his horse at breakneck
speed, shooting a staccatic volley. Hargreaves moved more
slowly.' (Afterwards Lispy revealed that Hargreaves's belt
buckle, glistening in the sun, had made an easy target.)

As nuclear weapons grew more destructive, however,
strategists in the United States came to appreciate that the duel
model was inappropriate and co-operation advantageous. The
United States and the Soviet Union now shared an interest in
avoiding mutual disaster. This dilemma posed sociologically

more interesting questions. Co-operation, negotiation and disarmament could benefit both, if the other could be trusted. In a non-zero-sum game, the winnings can be increased through co-operation. The problem, as Nasar (1998: 117) explains, was that co-operation appeared to demand an umpire, a Hobbesian sovereign, a World Government who could enforce disarmament on both sides, or (perhaps) a mediator trusted by both sides. This was not attractive to the United States, whose government was determined to live, in Locke's terms, in a state of nature.

John Nash solved the problem of co-operation in the absence of a sovereign by demonstrating that even where there is no umpire to enforce an agreement, non-zero-sum games can reach an equilibrium point, 'a situation in which no player could improve his or her position by choosing an alternative available strategy' (Nasar 1998: 97). If players can calculate their best strategy, they do not need an umpire to reach agreement. The problem identified by Hobbes and Locke had been solved, and the conditions under which reciprocal altruism will benefit both parties can potentially be identified.

A year after the theory's publication, the model of the *Prisoner's Dilemma* was devised to exemplify Nash's theory, and to explore when reciprocal altruism becomes a stable strategy. This famous parable uses the model of two suspects who have been arrested and are being interrogated in different rooms. The prisoner wonders whether he can trust the other to remain silent. Each is told that, if they alone implicate the other in the crime, they will be rewarded. If both confess, both will receive a moderate sentence, since their confession helped the police solve the crime. If one refuses to confess (i.e. refuses to 'defect'), even though the other has done so, his sentence will be heavier. If the other prisoner is suspected of having confessed, it will therefore be better to take the same course oneself (Trivers 1985: 389–90).[2] At first sight, the most rational plan seems to be to defect rather than trust the other prisoner to remain silent. Mutual defection is however more costly than co-operating with the other prisoner so both should remain silent. Each prisoner faces the dilemma that, although defection is less risky than co-operation, if both defect they will both do worse than if they had co-operated with each other. If Nash were correct, the game should produce an equilibrium point in which both prisoners use the strategy that gives them the best outcome available in the circumstances. If the other prisoner cannot be trusted, that would seem to be for both to confess.

Nasar (1998: 119) argues that the Prisoner's Dilemma refutes Adam Smith's claim that individuals pursuing their private interests will inevitably benefit the collective (in this case, the pair of prisoners as a group). The dilemma shows that if each prisoner pursues their immediate private interest every time they are arrested they do not achieve the best long-term outcome for themselves, let alone for the other prisoner. Here lies a solution to the war of each against all. Robert Axelrod realised that, even though co-operation may be preferable to short-term self-interest, it would only develop if the prisoners can anticipate each other's intentions (Axelrod 1990). Since they are secluded from one another in the cells, anticipation must be based on prior knowledge. If the game is played once, the stable strategy will be to defect, but if it is played repeatedly by the same players the stable strategy may be to co-operate through remaining silent. To rely on

---

[2] The actual rewards and punishments can be set at different values (compare Dawkins's 1976 account with Trivers's). The crucial feature is that they must be ranked so that the temptation to defect alone gives the highest 'payoff', followed by the reward of mutual silence, the punishment for mutual defection and last, the 'sucker's payoff' for remaining silent when the other defects.

co-operation, the prisoners must already have interacted with each other in ways that test their loyalty to one another. They must, in other words, have evidence of the other's commitment to reciprocal altruism. This provided a clear explanation for the desire to perpetuate social relationships out of self-interest, the condition envisaged by Locke. By simulating the game on a computer, Axelrod (1990: 42) found the most stable long-term strategy was one called 'Tit for tat'. In 'Tit for tat' the player begins by anticipating that the other will co-operate (not confess) and then, in subsequent moves, does what the other player did in their previous move. In this way other players who co-operate are rewarded, but those who defect are punished. The cumulative benefits of co-operation are greater than those of always confessing to the jailer, since mutual betrayal eliminates the reward for confession. If they are able to identify and pair off with trustworthy partners, those playing 'Tit for tat' can isolate those who play 'Always defect' and refuse to play with them.

This discovery can be extended to real life situations of reciprocal exchange where the return is delayed, and the dilemma is whether one can trust the other to make a return gift when one is in need. Make a gift on the first occasion, but withhold it on the second if it is not reciprocated. It explains how co-operation can evolve in a 'state of nature', even when it is in competition with selfishness.

The ideas developed by Nash, Axelrod and others show how people who renege on their reciprocal obligations, or fail to contribute to co-operation, are a threat to self-regulated social order. In the terms of commons management, they are the 'free-riders'. In a realistic situation, where people make mistakes, a strategy a little more forgiving than 'Tit for tat' may score even more highly. In fact, since the success of each strategy varies according to those played against it, increasingly generous strategies do better than others until eventually they themselves succumb to the short-term strategy 'Always defect', allowing 'Tit for tat' to succeed once more (Ridley 1996: 75–8). Social networks may thus expand or shrink according to the competing strategies in play at any time. Stable social situations, where people frequently interact with each other, provide the best context for trust and co-operation to develop.

The costs and benefits of each strategy depend on the resources being played for. Bruce Winterhalder (1996) emphasises that there may always be more than one strategy in play at any time. 'Tolerated theft' or 'scrounging', which has been observed in non-human species, can take place if an individual has so much of a resource that the surplus is not worth defending and scroungers are allowed to take some. The success of this strategy will depend on the proportion of scroungers to productive individuals (Vickery et al. 1991). The higher the frequency of scroungers the more are incentives to work productively threatened. Scrounging was rampant in Johannesburg and had become a real threat to social order. 'The easiest way to get the gold dust was – hop in and take it from some other fellow. Get him drunk first, or get him in an argument. No one cared what happened to him' (Kemp 1932: 24). Bonny McCay and James Acheson (1987) and Elinor Ostrom (1990) showed that, where the management of common property is concerned, self-regulation only works when scroungers ('free-riders') who over-exploit the commons can be detected and punished. There are two options. Everyone in the community may police their own partners in exchange, or authority (sovereignty) may be delegated to representatives of the community. Those who co-operate can probably never entirely eliminate free-riders who scrounge or renege on their obligations, but it is in their interests to minimise competing strategies if they are to get the fullest benefits from reciprocity

(Nowak and Sigmund 1998: 575). This is a strong incentive to maintaining social order, even in the simplest societies. If, however, conditions change so as to reduce people's expectation that they will need each other in future, or if the rewards of scrounging increase, the social order may break down.

Game theory and altruism

Robert Trivers's theory of reciprocal altruism built on the discoveries of game theory to explain the evolution of altruistic exchange between individuals who are not necessarily closely genetically related; to move, in other words, beyond the purely kin-selected form of altruism explained by Hamilton. If one individual temporarily has more of a resource than she or he needs, they may choose to share the surplus with another individual who is temporarily suffering a shortage. Trivers argues such behaviour will benefit both individuals if the debt is subsequently repaid. This pattern is most likely to develop where there is a risk of death, such as from starvation, and where it is impossible to predict which individual will be successful on any one occasion, yet those who *are* successful in obtaining food get more than their immediate need. Both partners will therefore survive whereas, on their own, both would probably soon have died. They are playing a non-zero-sum game. Hillard Kaplan and Kim Hill calculated the benefits of sharing food between households among the Ache hunter-gatherers of South America. They found sharing honey increases the food available to each household by 20 per cent, sharing of meat increases it by 40 per cent, while all observed food sharing increases the level of nutrition by 80 per cent (Kaplan and Hill 1985: 233; cf. Kaplan, Hill and Hurtado 1990). There can thus be strong incentives to honour reciprocal obligations, and the evolution of the mental skills required to keep track of such relations will be favoured by natural selection.

As Axelrod predicted in his study of the Prisoner's Dilemma, reciprocity will develop as partners learn to be trustworthy, and each expects their mutual dependence to continue indefinitely (Trivers 1985: 364). During human evolution, we have developed the complex cognitive skills required to track social relationships, reward those who honour their obligations to us and punish those who cheat. This kind of altruism only works when A knows he/she has a continuing social relationship with B, and that B is trustworthy. For this reason, reciprocal relationships are often framed in the *idiom* of kinship, even though such kinship is 'made up', or *fictive*. In the language of the Anangu of central Australia, for example, the word *walytja* means both a kinsperson and someone you care for (Goddard 1987). People who lived together as members of the same hunting and gathering band became *walytja*, both to each other and the country they jointly looked after. Cousins who grew up together called each other 'brother' and 'sister' (Layton 1997).

Reciprocal aid between households is also widespread in peasant societies. Every household needs to call on neighbours for help when a member falls ill, or crops fail through accident, but none can anticipate when it will need help in future (Erasmus 1996, Scott 1976, Panter-Brick 1993). Ethnicity is a form of fictive kinship on a larger scale, in the sense that it alleges relatedness based on common ancestry, or 'brotherhood'. The dynamics of ethnic communities are considered below.

Equilibrium points

The case of the Johannesburg gold rush illustrates how some social settings make it difficult to secure co-operation, leading to minimal levels of social order. Tilo Grätz (2002) describes gold miners in northern Benin, West Africa, as occupying a 'semi-autonomous social field'. The African miners are working illegally and are therefore reluctant to appeal to the state for arbitration during local disputes; a somewhat different situation to the South African gold rush, where the sought-after mining commissioner kept himself hidden. Here it is the gold miners who are deliberately placing themselves in Locke's state of nature: 'Men living together according to reason, without a common Superior on Earth with Authority to judge between them, is *properly the state of nature*' (Locke 1960: 280). Nonetheless, while there is violence, the miners do not live in the Hobbesian condition, a war of every man against every other man. The miners disregard the state's demands, but there are stable principles governing the sharing and distribution of yields from mining among themselves, for paying assistants and leasing houses and equipment, presumably because the costs of disregarding these principles take immediate effect.

Use-rights to shafts in the gold field are less stable and are the cause of most disputes. These are less easily resolved and miners do occasionally seek help from the local village headman. The headman has some authority among miners because each immigrant must find housing in a local village. An unruly miner can be forced to leave the village. Grätz identifies several incentives to accept the resolution of a dispute. Someone who fails to regain ownership of a shaft they had abandoned may accept some shares in the renewed operation, or exploit a new shaft. The supply of gold is evidently not finite; this is not a zero-sum game. Workers excluded from a team for antisocial behaviour can form their own team. Also, 'the permanent threat of governmental authorities to expel the miners . . . makes immigrant miners especially want to avoid longer processes of negotiation of a particular case and to accept a verdict in favour of maintaining the general and continued access to resources' (Grätz 2002: 17).

Frontier-like societies may exist in the midst of an otherwise well-regulated nation state. Dick Hobbs et al. (2003) investigated the policing of the night time economy of clubs and pubs in contemporary Britain. They argue that the state deliberately withdrew its authority to allow commercial interests to prosper. Local governments idealistically hoped that relaxed licensing laws would create city centres like those of continental Europe, where people thronged to pavement cafés, theatres and art galleries. Unfortunately English weather, the demolition of traditional city centres and the sense that city economies could only survive through cut-throat competition led to explosive growth in the number of bars and clubs catering largely for young people in the transitional life stage between childhood and adulthood. This set the scene for both high profits and a high level of disorder.

Hobbs et al. argue that the night is archetypically a time when the normal order is put aside (269). Since commercial interests have flocked to exploit the developing night club economy, including the sale of drugs, it is not surprising that some are criminal. As one bouncer remarked, there was certainly a continental atmosphere in the city, but it was the atmosphere of the Somme, not Paris. Hobbs et al. argue that the state has effectively abdicated responsibility for policing the night time economy, and private security has therefore been introduced to protect commercial interests. While the police retain sole authority and responsibility for patrolling public spaces, bars and night clubs are privately policed. The night time has become an enclave within the state that exists in Locke's state of nature.

Since policing clubs lies outside the scope of public authority, it relies on the threat of violence to be credible (there are no private law courts). Bouncers lack the authority of the state that police possess. The physical force used by door staff is often a response to the disorderly situations it is their job to resolve. Bouncer-to-customer relations are 'moral contests', but they are also interpersonal contests. Using a bouncer who does not look capable of violent enforcement 'could put *the sovereignty of the door* at risk' (Hobbs et al. 2003: 143, my emphasis). The state has sacrificed its monopoly over the control of force. Force has therefore become 'both dispersed and concentrated into the institutions of civil society' (Reyna: 2003: 265; chapter 3 returns to this phenomenon).

The overwhelming desire to prevent violence against customers, staff and bouncers must be balanced against commercial considerations in a very competitive market place, including the management's perception of the market niche the club is exploiting. Bouncers make decisions in a chaotic, noisy and confusing environment. 'Acceptable levels of disrespect, dishonour, and discourtesy are negotiated and renegotiated in the light of a few enforceable formal parameters of behaviour in an environment whose very existence as a commercial zone of liminality promotes transgression' (Hobbs et al. 2003: 161). The key problem is that of spotting free-riders who are unwilling to conform to minimal regulations of conduct in a context where only limited mutual trust can develop. The problem was exacerbated when drug gangs imposed their free-riding with arms.

Some problems in locating the 'state of nature'

Do these cases really constitute social life in Locke's state of nature? In one sense they do, since actors are frequently negotiating among themselves without recourse to a higher authority. On the other hand, they are generally using strategies that

already exist as part of their cultural repertoire and are therefore, in another sense, governed 'by the Customs or Laws
of the Country they live in' (Locke 1960: 321). Locke had
probably not appreciated that there could be 'settled rules'
outside the nation state. The peacekeeping roles of gold rush
Johannesburg were not created on a blank slate, but based on
a known repertoire (marshal, judge, jury). In northern Benin,
a meeting of all major shaft owners working at a particular site to resolve a dispute follows a traditional West African
procedure (cf. Bohannan 1958: 54–6 on the Tiv 'moot'). Grätz
writes that seeking the help of a village headman 'is transferred
from the general relationships between hosts and rural labour
migrants in the region and is also to be found in Burkina Faso
and elsewhere' (Grätz 2002: 10). Bourdieu demonstrates that
any interaction must take place within the idiom of a culture
if agents are to understand each other's intentions. People
rely upon their learned habitus (Bourdieu 1977: 72, 100–9)
or practical consciousness of appropriate strategies. 'Practical consciousness consists of knowing the rules and tactics
whereby daily life is constituted and reconstituted across time
and space' (Giddens 1984: 90).

People who renege on their reciprocal obligations, or fail to
contribute to co-operation, are a threat to self-regulated social
order. However, Johannesburg was not the only place that had
difficulty finding people willing to enforce the law. Identifying
and punishing free-riders is often unpleasant. There are some
excellent studies of self-government in European villages that
illustrate the problem. In rural León, northern Spain, the most
important office was that of elected *procurador* or village headman (Behar 1986). He organised collective work parties to
maintain village property. Many were reluctant to take on the
role since the occupant had to enforce fines on fellow villagers
who failed to join collective work parties (Behar 1986: 149). A
similar problem existed in the Swiss Alps, where officials were

elected to convene community assemblies, organise communal work parties to make good avalanche damage and so forth (Friedl 1974: 23).

Ruth Behar nonetheless gives a detailed account of how social order is negotiated by members of the community acting in their own interests. Tenure of newly created fields in her village of Santa María was allocated by drawing lots once the land was cleared, to prevent anyone working harder on the portion which would become their own (Behar 1986: 232–4). John Friedl records similar strategies in the Swiss village of Kippel. When a set of brothers build a house together in Kippel they allocate the finished apartments by lottery, to ensure no one puts more effort into the apartment they will acquire (Friedl 1974: 60–1). Families in the Swiss village of Törbel agree on the division of the family landholding into equal portions before drawing lots to determine who will receive each part (Netting 1981: 193–4). Lotteries are used in Pellaport, the French village I studied, to allocate wood from the communal forest and, in the past, portions of common meadow (Layton 2000: 59, 84). In every case, the opportunity for favouritism or appropriation by the powerful is eliminated. The inhabitants of both Kippel and Santa María rely on the rigorous application of rotas to ensure that each household can rest assured that every other one will make a fair contribution to work on behalf of the whole group (Friedl 1974: 55, Behar 1986: 203–5). Communal obligations and work parties persisted in Santa María 'as a result of the conscious agreement of villagers to be bound by them . . . The rules existed to insure that not merely the majority, but everyone would carry out their vicinal obligations . . . whether willing or reluctant' (Behar 1986: 185).

Confidence that one's efforts will not be undermined by free-riders is therefore essential, if the co-operation of equals is to be sustained. This confidence depends on knowledge that the community possesses reliable strategies to enable equitable access, to enforce compliance and to provide the opportunity to detect cheaters. When everyone lives and repeatedly inter-acts with one another in a nucleated village, it is relatively easy for each to check on whether their neighbours are living up to the community's standards. Gellner represented this local civil society as the tyranny of the community, of cousins and of ritual (Gellner 1994: 7). It is true that such mutual surveil-lance may be perceived as oppressive, but also clear that it is in everyone's long-term interests to sustain it. Once such an organised consensus breaks down, or free-riders can act with impunity, disorder is harder to control and units in civil society are at risk of disintegrating.

Limited forms of sovereignty

Hobbs et al. (2003: 143) wrote of the 'sovereignty' of the night club doorway. Harriet Rosenberg (1988: 39) and Robert Netting (1981: 78) have described alpine villages as miniature republics. There are many degrees of sovereignty and the state of nature is an ideal or extreme that lies beyond this contin-uum. Sovereignty does not necessarily imply a literal king. A republic can assert sovereignty. Sovereignty arises where indi-viduals have surrendered some of their autonomy, or agency, to another that acts on their behalf to regulate social relations. As soon as the Inuit agreed the Akudmirmiut leader should execute Padlu, the multiple murderer, they had conferred a minimal amount of sovereignty upon him. When the night club claims exclusive right to decide who shall enter, it is claim-ing to have appropriated a limited degree of sovereignty from the state. When those disputing ownership of a mine shaft among the Benin gold miners submit to the decision of the major shaft owners, they accept the sovereignty of influential men in their community. At times miners go beyond the mining community to seek the authority of village headmen.

The use of force is the ultimate sanction. Sovereignty may be conferred voluntarily or asserted as a right (this was the basis of the debate between Hobbes, Locke and Filmer), but force always underlies politics. It is most visible in the absence of an agreed authority. When the police, as representatives of the state, decline to regulate access to night clubs, the bouncers have only their own force to draw upon. When the representative of the state kept himself hidden during the Johannesburg gold rush, the local community was driven to persuade one of their own number to arrest Hargreaves's gang by force.

Anthony Giddens described the process through which agents are bound together in a social network as 'structuration' (Giddens 1984: 35). Agents cannot achieve their goals without the help of others. The individual's agency, or ability to act in ways of their own choice, is always limited by mutual dependence, whether through reciprocity or domination. The distribution of power in society both constrains and enables interaction, opening up some possibilities for agency while precluding others (Giddens 1984: 173). This was the phenomenon recognised by Morgenstern and von Neumann, but game theory only models a minimum number of players (or teams) interacting over a limited period. Structuration extends the insights of game theory to extensive social networks. It recognises that the actions of some people may influence the options open to others without the actor necessarily being aware of the others' presence. Structuration is a long-term process in which agents' actions either reproduce or transform their position in society, depending on whether the distribution of power is reinforced or destabilised.

If the sovereignty of the state is incomplete, is there a risk that the existing social order will break down? This is not necessarily so when the state has voluntarily delegated partial sovereignty, as in the case of local government. However, where the distribution of sovereignty is contested, the distribution of power will influence the stability of society. Here lies the origin of disorder, of anarchy in the negative sense of the term. Once recreational drug use became a feature of the British night time economy, drug dealers began to contest club and bar owners' partial sovereignty over their premises. Sovereignty was becoming increasingly dispersed, and social order was breaking down. In gold rush Johannesburg force was evenly distributed and the rewards of free-riding were so great that mutual trust had no opportunity to develop. Stephen Reyna (Reyna 2003) explains the repeated episodes of civil war in Chad in similar terms: the power to assert sovereignty has largely been wrested from the state, and competing local concentrations have been amassed among rebel groups within civil society.

A DARWINIAN APPROACH TO SOCIAL EVOLUTION

Progress versus adaptation

The manner in which agents' strategies transform the social environment in which other agents act can be modelled as an evolutionary 'fitness landscape'. So far in this chapter, evolutionary theory has been used to explain how stable patterns of co-operation and reciprocity can develop over time. How can evolutionary theory be used to explain change? Nineteenth-century social scientists' theory of evolution differed in important ways from Darwin's theory of natural selection (table 2.1). In the eighteenth and nineteenth centuries, social scientists thought of evolution as progressive: societies evolved from

Table 2.1 *Nineteenth-century theories of evolution*

19th-century social scientists	Darwin
evolution has a direction	evolution is random
change takes place at the level of the system	change takes place at the level of the individual
change is driven from within the system	change is caused by the pressures of the environment

simple to complex, human thought evolved from irrational to rational. Progressive change was taken to be normal.

At least some social scientists are still influenced by the nineteenth-century approach. Giddens, as was noted in chapter 1, rejects the use of evolutionary theory in the social sciences on the grounds that to succeed, the theory must achieve an impossible goal. It:

Must identify a [single?] mechanism of change, which must be linked to a sequence of changes in which types or aspects of social organisation replace each other, and the theory must work across the whole spectrum of human history. (1984: 232)

Giddens's characterisation of evolution makes implicit reference to the work of Herbert Spencer. Spencer considered that societies develop in the way individual animal or plant organisms grow. Just as the embryo begins as a small clump of undifferentiated cells and develops into a complex system of tissues and organs so, according to Spencer, the structure of human societies becomes increasingly differentiated through time (Spencer 1972 [1857]: 39). Spencer's ideas have long since been rejected, but some societies do change through time even if they don't all progress in the same direction. How can this be explained in terms borrowed from Darwinian theory? If a society is stable this must also be explained, rather than taken for granted or attributed to 'inertia'. Such tendencies can be explained through the recursive effects of 'positive' and 'negative' feedback during the structuration of social relationships.

Atomistic and systematic models

The introduction to this chapter noted that social scientists have continued to resist the individualistic bias of Darwinian evolutionary theory, on the grounds that social systems have emergent properties. The following section argues that at least some evolutionary theorists recognise the importance of interaction between organisms of the same or different species in understanding the rate and direction of evolution, and recognition of the emergent properties of *ecological* systems can therefore be incorporated into a Darwinian framework. It is plausible to think, by analogy, of social systems providing the ecology of individual action.

The preceding examples show that local communities do not necessarily depend upon a sovereign to prevent the war of every man against every other man. Stable strategies of co-operation and reciprocity can develop out of self-interest. The breakdown of social order cannot be attributed to a natural human anarchy breaking free as the state loosens its grip. A more sophisticated theory of social order is needed that places self-interest in the context of social interaction, in order to show why social order is sometimes sustained and at other times disrupted. Mark Duffield (2001: 28) makes a similar point in his analysis of disorder in Third World states. He points out that Dependency Theory (Gunder Frank 1971, Wallerstein 1974) acknowledged the way in which the powerful northern states exploit those in the south. Dependency theory fell out of favour and southern states are now commonly blamed for their own instability. Duffield argues that in doing so, the north refuses to acknowledge the impact of its dominant position in the world economic system. He sees current claims that southern states should develop their own civil society as a way of shifting the blame for social instability onto the victims of a global process driven by the north (Duffield 2001: 71).

This chapter will argue that the global economy is the social analogue of an ecological system, in which the costs and benefits of individuals' strategies are shaped by the niche they occupy in a changing system. It argues for an ecology of social behaviour that can account for the development of stable strategies over time, but can also assess whether some local social systems are inherently unstable or whether they are destabilised by changes in their larger social environment. It is, in other words, about the evolution of order and disorder in social systems. The biologist John Maynard Smith noted the power of the analogy between rational action and genetic adaptation in his work on the application of game theory to animal behaviour: the utility of a strategy in economics is analogous to the contribution a behaviour pattern makes to reproductive success in evolutionary theory. Rationality (seeking the strategy which best meets the individual's economic interests) is analogous to the process through which natural selection blindly acts upon alternative, genetically determined patterns of behaviour to favour the most adaptive variant (Maynard Smith 1982: vii, 2). As Nasar pointed out, the most favourable strategy may be determined by the state of interaction between individuals.

'Evolution', as used in this chapter, refers to Darwinian evolution, not progressive evolution in Herbert Spencer's sense, where social systems are driven by an internal dynamic toward ever-increasing complexity. In Darwinian theory the individual actor is the object of analysis, the 'unit of selection'. Change arises from the consequences of variation in individual behaviour in a specified environment. For humans, and for many other species, the environment is both *physical* and *social*. In neo-Darwinian theory, random genetic variation creates a variety of bodily form and behaviour within a population. Environmental conditions determine which varieties are better able to reproduce and raise offspring to maturity than alternative forms, and it is the genes responsible for the successful variants that are passed on to the next generation in greatest numbers. In the social theory of Bourdieu and Giddens it is learned cultural strategies that are transmitted with greater or lesser frequency during social interaction.

Selfish genes and their ecology

The following paragraphs discuss whether the natural environment has emergent properties, similar to those of social systems, which arise from the interaction of different organisms. Concluding that this is the case, it is argued that ecological systems provide better models of process than the simplistic concepts of development and function on which Herbert Spencer relied.

There are two extremes in contemporary neo-Darwinian theory, the 'selfish gene' and the 'fitness landscape' schools. These competing ideas have generated debate in evolutionary theory as to whether the primary motor of evolutionary change is the gene, or the ecological system that exerts selective pressures on the organism. The debate parallels a problem in social theory. Should analysis focus solely on the individual decision-maker, as in classical economics, or note that the outcome of his decisions is determined by the emergent properties of social interaction highlighted in game theory and structuration? In genetics, Richard Dawkins (1976) advocates the 'selfish gene', whose only 'goal' is to ensure it is transmitted to future generations, regardless of its effect on the organism that carries it. Dawkins does acknowledge that genes interact with one another within the developing organism (Dawkins 1976: 271), but this is incidental to his general argument. The biologists Stuart Kauffman (1993) and Simon Conway Morris (1998), on the other hand, argue that the environment to which organisms adapt is transformed by other organisms.

Leigh Van Valen showed one cause of progressive change, the 'Red Queen' scenario (Van Valen 1973). Here a predator population and its prey become increasingly specialised, as each exercises a selective effect on variation in the other. Cheetahs preying on gazelles favour survival of the fastest gazelles by killing those who are slower. This in turn exerts a selective pressure on cheetahs, favouring the fastest hunters. Conway Morris (1998) explains the Cambrian explosion of diverse early life forms around 550 million years ago as a consequence of the appearance of the first predators undermining existing adaptations. Suddenly, there was huge selective pressure favouring those organisms that could evade or repel predators, leading to a proliferation of new species. Hence, contrary to the thrust of Dawkins's approach, the interaction of organisms is acknowledged to shape the direction in which any population evolves. Kauffman writes, 'In co-evolutionary processes, the fitness of one organism or species depends upon the characteristics of the other organisms or species with which it interacts, while all simultaneously adapt and change' (Kauffman 1993: 33). Kauffman extends this principle to the co-evolution of genes in the organism; it is in genes' 'self-interest' to 'co-operate', to ensure the organism survives long enough to reproduce. It is at this point that game theory and structuration become relevant to evolution.

A fitness landscape is a theoretical model that represents adaptation in an evolving population. Populations climb peaks in their landscape as they become increasingly well adapted to a particular ecological niche. If there were no interaction between species during biological evolution, each population would eventually stabilise on the highest peak in its landscape, eliminating fellow members stranded on lower peaks (the 'selfish gene' or neo-classical view in economics). In practice, however, the reproductive success of each species is partly determined by the fitness of other species such as predators, with which it interacts, and which change the shape of the landscape.

Adam Smith's theory of economics can be compared to the 'selfish gene' approach in evolutionary biology. The butcher, the brewer and the baker pursue their self-interest independently of one another, but we have their self-interested activities to thank for our daily meat, beer and bread. Marx's critique of Smith relied on what can, in retrospect, be regarded as a 'landscape' approach that recognises positive feedback. Individuals competing for their self-interest differentially affect each other's life chances, creating the industrial equivalent of an ecological system. A 'selfish gene' model implies, as does neo-classical economics, that genetic variability will eventually stabilise around the best available adaptation to the ecological niche and does not predict cumulative change of the sort addressed by Marx in his model of class conflict arising from the Industrial Revolution.

The concept of evolutionary landscapes was first explicitly used in the social sciences in Richard Nelson and Sidney Winter's evolutionary theory of economics. According to the evolutionary theory of economics the 'rationality' of behaviour is not measured in terms of the individual's intentions (as in classical economics), but in terms of the outcome for the business or individual's *economic* survival in an environment that contains competing firms or individuals (Nelson and Winter 1982). When a firm searches for innovations it is not perfectly informed about all possible alternatives, but draws at random from techniques similar to those it already uses. The consequences of any choice are not fully known. Different firms respond differently to the same 'murky signals' in the economic environment (Nelson and Winter 1982: 276), allowing a range of behaviours to be explored across the industry as a whole. Innovations put into practice also transform the landscape within which other firms are operating. In the global economy, the 'fitness' of local social strategies is thus determined by interaction with other players.

Selection and cultural continuity or change

Human social behaviour is determined by a combination of genetically determined and culturally learned strategies. Schools of thought differ on the relative strength of the ingredients. Social theorists such as Giddens minimise the genetic component, evolutionary psychologists minimise the cultural component, while behavioural ecologists and dual inheritance theorists give a substantial role to both (Laland and Brown 2002). The relative weight that should be attributed to genes and culture in human social behaviour has been hotly debated. The evolutionary psychologists Lida Cosmides and John Tooby have accused social scientists of treating the mind as an empty vessel, to be filled with learned social rules. Cosmides and Tooby's main targets are Durkheim and the US cultural anthropologist Clifford Geertz (Cosmides, Tooby and Barkow 1992: 25–8). Cosmides and Tooby argue the opposite case: evolution has given the human mind a complex structure with many specific skills which enable the individual to decide, for example, whom to mate with, when to co-operate with others and how much parental care to expend on each offspring (Cosmides, Tooby and Barkow 1992: 73). Human cognition has a standard design that emerged from the selective pressures experienced by hunter-gatherers (64). Modern variation only occurs in 'minor, superficial, nonfunctional traits' (Cosmides, Tooby and Barkow 1992: 38, cf. 78).

While the capacity we possess for constructing social relationships is undoubtedly genetically determined, the content of these relationships is cultural. Given the manifest variability in features such as social kinship, I prefer the approach taken by behavioural ecologists that acknowledges that local adaptations in social behaviour are generally achieved through learned strategies.

The fact that specific social strategies are learned does not preclude the probability that over time strategies that favour individual survival in society will tend to displace less adaptive strategies. If such strategies demand co-operation or reciprocity, self-interest can generate social order and an evolutionary theory of social interaction is possible. To the extent that social strategies are learned, Darwinian natural selection must however be treated as an analogy, not a cause of social change. Where a Darwinian approach is applied to culture, a mechanism for the 'selection' and transmission of learned traits, analogous to differential reproductive success and transmission of genetic traits, must therefore be identified (Elster 1983: 22). Perhaps those who happen by chance to use better-adapted artefacts, or social strategies such as particular types of fictive kinship, have greater reproductive success than do those who use less appropriate variants. The traits are transmitted when their children unconsciously copy the parents' behaviour. In this view, variants arise by chance, through imperfect copying (see discussions in Basalla 1988:

135–9, Elster 1983: 10). Intentional choice may speed up the rate at which more efficient strategies are adopted, but it is the consequences of people's choices that determine the strategies' viability, not the actor's intentions. Following Nelson and Winter (1982: 10–11), Basalla (1988) and Elster (1983) conclude that cultural change actually arises through a combination of random and intentional behaviour. In a stable situation, copying the tried and tested strategies of the previous generation is less risky than innovation (Boyd and Richerson 1985: 95ff). When the actor is uncertain, and does not know the probability of alternative outcomes arising from a course of action, choices between actions become increasingly random (Elster 1983: 70–6). We need not assume social change is always driven by far-sighted consciousness, merely by actors favouring social strategies that appear to give the best outcome available under local circumstances (Layton 2000).

The fitness landscape as a model for social change

In order to understand why local forms of civil society persist or dissolve, one must consider both their appropriateness to local conditions, and the impact upon them of changes in the wider social environment. Dawkins compared the spread of 'memes' (learned patterns of behaviour) to the spread of selfish genes, somewhat like an epidemic. W. H. Durham is a leading exponent of the 'dual inheritance' approach that argues genes and culture both influence each other's evolution (Laland and Brown 2002: 281). Durham objects that the epidemic model is based on 'radical individualism' and generally ignores power and coercion, which are emergent properties of social interaction that can influence the course of natural selection. 'In cultural systems . . . significant evolutionary forces can and do arise from unequal social relations' (Durham 1991: 182–3).

Peasants of El Salvador and Honduras overexploit a rugged environment, not through lack of education or concern, but because during the nineteenth century the landed elite had manipulated national land tenure policies, squeezing peasants out of productive land and annexing the good land for their own purposes (Durham 1991: 362; cf. Migdal 1988: 63 on land reform in Mexico). This is consistent with the ecological approach to natural evolution advocated by Kauffman and Conway Morris. James Scott (1976) showed how the 'Green Revolution', which introduced new high-yielding varieties of rice to Asian farmers, in some cases exacerbated divisions between the relatively prosperous and poorer peasants. This happened where only the relatively wealthy could afford the chemical fertilisers and the hired labour or simple machinery needed to cultivate 'Green Revolution' crops successfully. While the 'Green Revolution' varieties gave a better yield in the long run if properly cultivated, they could fail once every five years. A wealthy peasant might have sufficient financial resources to survive, but the greater long-term yield would be no use to a poorer peasant household forced out of production by starvation in the fifth year. 'Susceptibility' to innovation is therefore not randomly distributed. If a few are 'infected' with an innovation they change the shape of the evolutionary landscape and may make it *harder* rather than easier for others to adopt it. The social landscape has been transformed by others' agency. Durham, in the example cited above, similarly pointed out that the powerful may compel the weak to act, not in their own interests but in the interests of the powerful. To take these interactive processes into account demands an ecological approach to social evolution.

Some years ago a study of alternative ways of exploiting Peruvian rain forest showed that local hunters and horticulturalists collect produce worth roughly £452 per hectare per year without harming the forest. Cattle ranching in the same area would only yield £95 per hectare per year while logging all saleable timber would yield a one-off income of £645 (Peters, Gentry and Mendelsohn 1989). The indigenous adaptation is clearly the most productive. The problem for the state is that none of the foragers' and horticulturalists' yield enters the market and therefore it cannot be taxed to fund state activities. From the state's perspective the forest is 'dormant wealth lying about in almost criminal uselessness' (the phrase used by T. E. Day to describe central Australia in the early twentieth century). The state is therefore likely to use its power to favour ranching or logging.

Adaptation and alternative strategies

The idea of evolution as progress was so deeply rooted in nineteenth-century European thought that Darwin had to write notes to himself not to refer to higher and lower forms of life (Trivers 1985: 31–2, Laland and Brown 2002: 65). Grabher and Stark (1998: 57) point out that what they call the 'neo-liberal transition model' of post-socialist change in Eastern Europe embodies the kind of one-way, progressive evolution associated with Spencer and Comte, against which Darwin struggled (cf. Duffield 2001: 161). The neo-liberal transition model fails to explain the divergent outcomes of implementing a free market in different countries. Smith and Pickles (1998) make the same point. Western governments thought the introduction of a market economy, privatisation of property and democratisation of political life in former socialist states would proceed as a simple matter of diffusing more rational or advanced forms of organisation into societies that had been retarded by socialism: an application of the 'epidemic' model.

A realistic 'fitness landscape' has many dimensions, reflecting the many forces exerting selective pressure on a population. There are many conflicting pressures to adapt to various environmental constraints or opportunities. No individual organism or firm can adapt perfectly to all of them, and there can therefore be several sub-optimal but equally adaptive variants in a population living side by side. Social change is not necessarily a one-way process and no social institutions are universally the best or 'most evolved'.

Elizabeth Dunn documents a striking example of a sustainable alternative socio-economic system practised by Mormons in the United States. Mormon farmers are 'tithed', and their contributions go anonymously into cooked and preserved food that can only be distributed charitably within the church. Mormons discourage dependence on state welfare but 'the church recognizes that unforeseeable circumstances sometimes force people to rely on others for assistance in meeting basic needs' (Dunn 1996: 29). Free-riding is not allowed: 'Recipients should be actively searching for ways to improve their situations.' However poor, recipients are expected also to give. Direct repayment is not expected; when former recipients are back on their feet they give, not as reciprocation, but as fresh giving. As Dunn writes, 'It is the direct opposite of time and labour which is exchanged for wages' (31). Mormons pride themselves on being model citizens, but see their practices as steps in the direction of *their* ideal society, away from negative consequences of capitalism. 'The Mormons seek to expand their "civil society" (although this is not a term they would use) not by opposing the state, but by creating an alternative domain to the state' (Dunn 1996: 46, her parenthesis).

John Eidson and Gordon Milligan (2003: 47) note that one of the surprising results of privatisation in the former Soviet bloc is the survival of the legal successors to the collective farms of the socialist era as voluntary producer co-operatives. Many family-based farms have been set up in former East

Germany since reunification, but in 2001 over 50 per cent of arable land in the new federal states was still cultivated by co-operative or corporate farms, most of which were the successors to socialist co-operatives. Co-operatives have access to more capital than family farms, and their managers are often experienced entrepreneurs whose parents were middle-class peasants prior to collectivisation.

Processing co-operatives making cheese, wine and other agricultural products are also common in France, where they operate alongside private enterprises. Processing co-operatives are widely promoted by the French government as a means of ensuring the viability of family farms. Dairy associations have existed since 1264 in the part of Franche Comté where I conducted fieldwork (Lambert 1953: 175; see also Latouche 1938, Lebeau 1951). These associations made it possible to pool the milk of several households and produce large, hard cheeses that could be sold to merchants for export to other parts of France. During a period of economic uncertainty around the time of the First World War, many associations ceased co-operative production of cheese and handed over responsibility for making and selling cheeses to entrepreneurs. In most cases the building fortunately remained the property of the association or the village commune. The disadvantages of entrepreneurial production became apparent during the German occupation of the Second World War, when many entrepreneurs, like shopkeepers, profited from the clandestine sale of dairy produce on the black market, and kept the money for themselves (Lambert 1953: 176). After the liberation there was a widespread movement in Franche Comté to restore co-operative control over the production and marketing of cheese. Although entrepreneurs retained control in some villages, their actions are limited by competition with neighbouring co-operatives to provide the best price for milk, and the knowledge that they, too, could lose their position. Entrepreneurs and co-operatives shape each other's strategies and co-exist rather like different species in the same economic landscape.

An interesting case where the co-existence of two modes of organisation proved unsustainable is the development of the 'second economy' in Hungary during the final years of the socialist regime and the consequent weakness of private enterprise. Hann (1990) describes how workers in Hungarian state firms set up small private enterprises that could profit from the shortcomings in state production and distribution. The state tacitly encouraged this. However, the second economy was symbiotic with or even parasitic on the state economy, because workers borrowed equipment and diverted supplies of materials from their principal state employer. Moreover, the success of the second economy tended to weaken commitment to less well-paid work in normal working hours. Hann argues the collapse of socialism was partly due to people's unwillingness to adhere to one ideology during daytime and another (free enterprise) in the evenings. However, the collapse of the state command economy weakened the capacity of small enterprises to function, because of their dependence on the 'parent' state firm. Once the parent firm collapsed, its dependent enterprises were starved of resources. This seems a little like ivy strangling the tree it grows upon! It helps to explain the weakness of the East European market economy that Gellner decried.

CONCLUSION

This chapter has argued for Locke's broad conception of civil society. Civil society can develop without the aid of a sovereign or centralised state. People can come together to co-ordinate the peaceful pursuit of their own 'projects' (Gouldner 1980) without the intervention of a higher authority. As Locke argued, self-interest can itself create social order. Locke's state of nature is an ideal and there are many limited forms of sovereignty. The state may willingly delegate or passively acquiesce in the transfer of limited sovereignty to local communities. The Hobbesian notion that the state alone prevents local communities from dissolving into a war of every man against every other man is inaccurate, although contested sovereignty relies on a visible threat of violence and war may begin if mutual trust breaks down. Where the state or local civil society does fragment, the reasons are therefore likely to be found either in the dynamics of structuration, as the consequences of past social interaction influence future behaviour, or in changes in the social and economic environment. There is no doubt that our ability to keep track of social relationships and assess others' trustworthiness is genetically determined, but human social behaviour is flexible. We can change our social strategies according to circumstances, and those circumstances can be represented as a socio-economic environment whose evolutionary trajectory is the emergent outcome of enacting strategies. An increase in free-riding or scrounging can undermine co-operation and reciprocity. The causes of breakdown in the social order are discussed in the next chapter.

CHAPTER 3

The breakdown of social order

This chapter addresses two questions: what turns civil society against the state? What causes co-operation and reciprocity within civil society to give way to competition and conflict? The analysis is based on a combination of two theoretical approaches, the social theory of Pierre Bourdieu and Anthony Giddens, and the applications of game theory developed by behavioural ecologists. Bourdieu and Giddens, whose ideas are mentioned in chapter 2, were critical of two preceding schools of thought in social science. They argued for a synthesis that would acknowledge the strengths of both, but overcome the weaknesses of each school. On one hand there was a sociological tradition that considered individuals to be embedded in a social system, not free agents (classically represented in anthropology by Durkheim 1938 and Radcliffe-Brown 1952). According to this school, we are born into a society that allocates us to pre-determined social roles, so that everyone plays their part in sustaining the social order. Bourdieu and Giddens objected to this school's tendency to imply that social systems were inherently stable, and that individuals' interests were subordinated to the needs of society (Bourdieu 1977: 5, Giddens 1984: 25). Such 'structural' analysis also tended to render variation in individual performances as deviations from an unwritten score (the roles that individuals play on behalf of society), but Bourdieu argued that these roles are in fact sociological constructs built by the analyst. Both Bourdieu and Giddens argued that social order emerges spontaneously through interaction. The existence of a social system is not evidence that actors are striving to achieve it, nor is it evidence there is a supra-organic entity, 'society', that tries to maintain its own structure.

At the other extreme, the game theorists treated individuals as strategists acting solely in their own self-interest and constructing social relationships where none had previously existed (Blau 1964, von Neumann and Morgenstern 1944). Bourdieu and Giddens were opposed to treating actors as completely rational, playing the pure strategies of game theory. Instead, they argued, people should be viewed as *agents* seeking to shape their own future, but playing culturally specific strategies they have learned as children and reproduce (or modify) as adults. Each social tradition has its own distinctive strategies, which have been shaped by trial and error so that they converge on 'objective conditions' (Bourdieu 1977: 109). Bourdieu used the word 'habitus' to describe the social practices we learn as children and act out as adults.

The middle way advocated by Giddens and Bourdieu contended that social systems are created by the interaction of agents using cultural strategies that have been negotiated over successive generations. Participants in social exchange experience social life as a sequence of transactions, each of which is prompted by the previous offering and seeks to influence subsequent exchanges (Bourdieu 1977: 25). Agents make sense of what is happening through what Giddens called their practical consciousness, but they are unlikely to be fully aware of the ramifications of their own decisions upon others in the community. Agents' activities frequently reproduce the conditions that continue to make those activities possible. 'Each of the various forms of constraint are thus also, in varying ways, forms of enablement' (Giddens 1984: 173). Sometimes, however, agents' strategies undermine the preconditions that enabled them, making social change unavoidable (Giddens 1984: 170).

While I find Bourdieu's and Giddens's approach helpful, I consider their rejection of evolutionary theory unnecessary. Behavioural ecology can help to identify the circumstances that bring about social change; specifically, the conditions under which the existing social order of the nation state is weakened sufficiently to allow competing organisations in civil society to gain greater prominence. Game theory and the Prisoner's Dilemma can explain why agents sometimes change strategies, and how the new strategies transform the wider social system through the often unintended effects of structuration. Agents' strategies are directed toward managing or controlling resources in the social environment, and the model of the fitness landscape provides a way of representing how particular strategies can sometimes provide stable solutions to social living, yet at other times be undermined by shifts in the distribution of resources. The neo-Darwinian approach investigates the relative advantage of alternative behaviours for the reproductive success of an individual within a given environment. Just as any population contains genetic variability, so there are likely to be competing social strategies in play in any human community. There may, for example, always be some cheating in a system of reciprocal altruism (Vickery et al. 1991, Winterhalder 1996). Changes in the distribution of resources in the social environment may undermine the previously dominant strategy and allow subordinate ones to prosper.

Chapter 2 identified two simple and well-established models for explaining the breakdown of co-operation: firstly the transition from a non-zero-sum game to a zero-sum game, and secondly the inability to generate mutual trust when faced with the Prisoner's Dilemma. Both models underline the fact that human agency is expressed in a social environment, where the availability of information and material resources determine the most effective strategy to adopt in particular circumstances. They help explain what turns civil society against the state, and why co-operation within civil society may give way to competition and conflict.

Chapter 2 showed that people normally value social relationships and do not readily repudiate them. Even in the most elementary and seemingly anarchic social situations, people negotiate ways of upholding social interaction. When Alex de Waal studied the impact of famine on the peasant farmers of the Darfur region of the Sudan, he was surprised to find that people were more afraid that famine would erode the social relationships on which everyone depended for mutual aid than they were of suffering physical hunger (de Waal 1989). If the existing social order is to persist, however, it must be economically sustainable. Locally adaptive strategies can be undermined by transformations in the 'fitness landscape' brought about by neighbouring agents following competing strategies, and by outside intervention. If humans attach so much importance to social relations, why do people connive in disrupting and destroying the existing social order? I argue that the existing social order breaks down when changes in the economic and social fitness landscape undermine the effectiveness of previously dominant social organisations and empower other strategies, often ones that already exist as subordinate parts of the cultural repertoire. The distribution of force may drift away from the state and become concentrated in competing organisations within civil society.

In the first part of chapter 3, several causes of social instability are identified. Given the level of income created in their market economy and the state's limited ability to collect tax revenue, some African states cannot afford to sustain the bureaucratic government they inherited from the colonial era. Internal difficulties are exacerbated by international politics and economics. Many recent ethnographic studies of social disorder implicate globalisation and structural adjustment programmes in the erosion of the nation state's ability to fulfil its social contract with citizens. Even in impoverished societies, however, control of the state may still be a prize worth winning, particularly if foreign aid is channelled through the government, encouraging civil war in the scramble to gain control of government resources. Privatisation of common land held by local communities or lineages enables the rise of a landowning elite and, more importantly, destroys the local traditional civil society, as it did in England. Shifts in the local distribution of power also occur where foreign agents seek to gain control of valuable mineral resources. All these conditions make it increasingly difficult to sustain existing social networks.

The second part of the chapter exemplifies the two ways of analysing the breakdown of mutual trust that were identified in chapter 2. Robert Axelrod described how, if an end to mutual dependence can be foreseen, partners in reciprocal exchange will succumb to the temptation to defect from the relationship. Game theory predicts that, if players perceive that they have moved from a non-zero-sum game where co-operation increases the players' gains, to a zero-sum game where resources are fixed, co-operation will give way to competition. 'Loose molecules', young men who have lost work as a result of structural adjustment or the destruction of rural civil society, can be harnessed to new social movements that increase the power of aspiring leaders. Following Bourdieu and Giddens, however, the actual strategies available to agents are part of the local cultural repertoire. The trajectory of social process will depend to some extent on the character of those strategies. Case studies from Indonesia, India, Yugoslavia, Albania and Somalia show how, in particular cultural traditions, ethnicity and kinship provide the basis for excluding former partners in citizenship through the construction of a more restricted network of social relations, often violently enacted.

Revolutions never completely destroy existing social institutions. Examination of actual cases of radical social change suggests there is in fact always some degree of continuity in social practice, even where local communities face acute dispossession. The breakdown of social order rarely if ever results in total anarchy or asociality, but rather precipitates a shift between existing strategies, or the harnessing of current strategies to new ends (see, for example, the analysis of the French Revolution in McAdam, Tarrow and Tilly 2001: 53–8). Social change may be peaceful, but violence is likely when change threatens the position of social groups who have the power to resist, particularly where armed force is relatively evenly distributed between competing factions.

CAUSES OF BREAKDOWN OF SOCIAL ORDER

The cost of government

Bureaucracy has the potential to dissolve local allegiances and build up loyalty to the state. From the perspective of a colonising power, bureaucratisation provides a rational strategy to erode pre-colonial loyalties. Local leaders whose authority derives from an ethnic or kin-based constituency can be replaced by state appointees. Wealth extracted by local leaders as tribute is redirected to the state as taxation. Such changes not only empower central government, they provide a way of satisfying citizens that the state is honouring its social contract to represent all sections of the community.

The cost of government can, however, contribute to the vulnerability of social systems. Bureaucracy is more expensive than traditional government. Charles Tilly calculated that in 1600 the average Frenchman worked 50 hours per year to generate revenue for the state, but in 1966 he worked 650 hours (Tilly 1981: 203–4, cited in Migdal 1988: 16). Many states lack the means to extract this level of taxation, even if sufficient were available in the market economy.

In his book *The theory of social and economic organisation* the sociologist Max Weber contrasts bureaucratic and what he calls 'traditional' (feudal) government. Weber was more familiar with bureaucracy than with traditional government, and uncompromisingly regarded bureaucracy as the rational alternative. He relied on a theory of evolution as universal progress rather than local adaptation, akin to the approach of Herbert Spencer reviewed in chapter 2. The irrationality of traditional government lay, for Weber, in the chief's freedom to confer 'grace' on his subjects according to his personal pleasure or displeasure, quite arbitrarily (Weber 1947: 342). The chief's officials may be rewarded with rights in land, or portions of the taxes they collect, or payment from the chief's personal treasury. Traditional government has no regular system of appointments and promotions, and no regular technical training is required before assuming office. In a bureaucratic system, on the other hand, the rights and duties of office are explicitly spelt out through a rational legal system. Staff are appointed solely for their personal ability, and are professionally trained. Office holders owe their loyalty to the system, not to individual superiors. The income needed to pay salaries is raised through universal taxation.

The cost of implementing bureaucracy in the colonial states of Africa reveals that traditional government can also be rational, in circumstances where insufficient income is available to fund bureaucracy. Traditional government is associated with peasant-based societies where the majority of production is for subsistence and there is limited development of the market required to generate money for taxes. The two forms of government can therefore be interpreted as adaptations to different social circumstances, rather than steps on a ladder of progress toward complete rationality. In colonial Africa a complex bureaucracy was superimposed on societies based largely on subsistence farming. Commercial farming and mining were introduced to supply the colonising countries with raw materials and generate cash to finance colonial government, but such exports are vulnerable to international prices. The salaries paid to expatriate government officials were comparable to those paid in the home countries (Britain, France or Belgium) and when African officials took over they received the same salaries, without the productive base needed to sustain them. The disparity with the income of ordinary peasants was immense, making access to post-colonial government jobs a prize worth fighting for.

The British colonial administration began to bureaucratise government in southern Uganda in 1905, imposing a tax to finance British administrative activities (Fallers 1956). Local kings were restyled 'county chiefs'. In 1938, the British began to move county chiefs around, to break their traditional ties with followers. Because this also destroyed the traditional constraint on a chief's power – his reliance on popular support – a new system of advisory councils had to be introduced but, according to Beattie (1961), commoners were unable to accept the idea of advising their superiors and the councils were ineffective. Village headmen in Uganda also suffered. They were traditionally more dependent on personal contacts to maintain their authority than were higher chiefs. The British deprived village headmen of the right to collect tribute but could not provide them with an adequate alternative source of income, because the colony's economy was unable to generate a sufficient surplus to be taken in taxes.

If the state cannot deliver security and services, then local allegiances can be more effective, provoking the rise of small-scale patronage and the resurgence of kin-based or ethnic identities. Elizabeth Eames, discussing government in Nigeria, notes that in a traditional rural economy based on swidden agriculture, in which junior members of a local lineage could readily move on to open new fields in the forest, the use of patronage to retain their loyalty was widespread (Eames 1990: 41). Patronage is therefore part of the habitus that informs politics in many parts of Africa. Paul Richards argues that patrimonialism (localised patronage) is also compatible with various Western institutions, including the informal networking and brokerage activities of multinational companies, and therefore likely to continue in urban contexts (Richards 1996: 35).

For a social order to persist, it must be economically sustainable. In the post-colonial state of Chad, however, the government has five times 'had its domination unravel *as taxes were not paid, officials went unpaid*, roads crumbled, schools closed, and legal cases went unheard' (Reyna 2003: 270, my emphasis). The history of Chad is hence one of governments unable to control rebel movements. Nobody in Chad, Stephen Reyna reports, desired this instability. Richards similarly argues that the state controls insufficient resources to implement democracy and bureaucracy in Sierra Leone. Richards links the outbreak of civil war in Sierra Leone to the decline in state revenue during the 1990s. Not only had world recession reduced the price of many raw materials, countries such as Sierra Leone had exhausted some of their best supplies of minerals, particularly diamonds (Richards 1996: 36). The government therefore attempted to bolster support through patronage of rural, often educationally disadvantaged groups (Richards 1996: 40). However, given the shortage of resources in Sierra Leone, even patronage can never benefit everyone. The losers can see the inequity of the existing system. In Sierra Leone, alternative parties in the civil war struggle to implement an equitable system but lack the resources to do so; they only have the resources to erode the existing order, pushing society toward anarchy. Power remains personalised rather than organised into stable, hierarchical government because the forest environment restricts communication and the movement of armies (Little 1966: 65–6, Richards 1996: 80). Subsistence production depends heavily on groups of young men who perform various labour-intensive tasks in self-regulating gangs under the patronage of elders. But the traditional networks of patronage in civil society are unstable, partly because leaders compete to recruit a workforce.

Globalisation

The instability of bureaucratic government is not solely due to a shortage of local revenue. Using the model of fitness landscapes, chapter 2 illustrated how locally sustainable social systems can be undermined by competition from more powerful societies. Mark Duffield similarly argues that the increasing frequency of large-scale, complex disasters since the 1980s is not due to local conditions but a consequence of emerging global interdependence, exemplified by globalisation of the economy (Duffield 1994: 50–1). When resources are redirected away from local society to service the global economy, local social interaction begins to look like a zero-sum game. The risk of a scramble to gain a slice of what remains locally available increases, bringing different strategies to the fore.

Western-imposed 'structural adjustment' policies that limit the amount of money a state can spend on services to its citizens are repeatedly implicated in the recent breakdown of state government. Liberal economic reform has destroyed bureaucratic governments and reduced the competence of the nation state (Duffield 2001: 9). The disintegration of Yugoslavia, for example, was precipitated by the country's increasing economic dependence on foreign banks. The 'oil crisis' of the 1970s led Western banks to extend large-scale credit to Yugoslavia, as to other East European and Third World countries. By the late 1970s, 85 per cent of Yugoslavian investment depended on foreign loans (Denich 2003). This dependency was revealed in the early 1980s, when Western banks began demanding repayment on their investments. The International Monetary Fund obliged Yugoslavia to meet repayments by reducing domestic spending and instead earning money from exports. Free to travel, Yugoslavs had been aware that their standard of living was only slightly below that of Western Europe, but that standard now began visibly to fall (Vucho 2002: 55). Aleksander Vucho argues that the failure of the ruling oligarchy to resolve the economic crisis of the mid-1980s made people willing to accept the craziest person as leader, because he offered a simple and quick solution. Milosevic exploited ethnic tensions in the countryside to further his sectarian goals (see chapter 1). NATO sanctions, imposed in 1992 to punish Milosevic, had greatest impact on the urban citizens who were closest to the West, turning them from opponents of Milosevic into his supporters in the competition to secure the largest slice of visibly diminishing resources in what had become a zero-sum game (Vucho 2002: 67–8; cf. Jansen 2000).

Johanna Lessinger argues that recent conflict between Hindus and Muslims in India is less about religion than about class conflict that has been generated by the strains of globalisation (Lessinger 2003: 168). Repayment of foreign debts caused a balance of payments crisis and inflation. As the government abandoned support for textile and other local industries, male employment declined and female employment, often in the informal sector, grew. Gender relations were transformed. Economic liberalisation threatened to dismantle many forms of government social security (Rao and Reddy 2001). India's petty bourgeoisie and rural landowners also felt they had been excluded from the rise of consumer culture. The caste hierarchy was breaking down, and this was perceived as a threat by members of higher castes. In the early 1980s, a group of low-caste people from one village in south India tried to break free by converting to Islam. Hindu organisations used this event to mobilise the Hindutva movement, which campaigns to replace India's secular constitution with a Hindu-based state that will support the traditional order (cf. McAdam, Tarrow and Tilly 2001: 148).

Privatisation and the destruction of local civil society

The original privatisation movement, the English enclosures, was justified by the claim that private property is better managed than collective property (see chapter 1). Since the debate prompted by Garrett Hardin's *Tragedy of the commons* (Hardin 1968, McCay and Acheson 1987, Ostrom 1990) some writers now accept that local control of the commons is sustainable and that local communities may be better equipped than other organisations to manage water or forest (Benda-Beckmann 2001: 296). Yet, despite this evidence, the economic property rights school continues to assume that only private ownership and freely transferable use-rights give security of tenure and therefore contribute to economic profitability (Duffield 2001: 101), creating the particular kind of civil society extolled by Ernest Gellner and Adam Seligman.

In the traditional kingdom of Bunyoro, the British attempted soon after colonisation to replace the feudal hierarchy of rights to land with private smallholdings for each household (Beattie 1961). Traditional administrative officials, better informed about the new legislation than householders, registered their benefices as private property. Peasants suddenly discovered that they had become tenants, just as happened in parts of France during the 1790 revolution, where peasants complained that they had lost a seigneur but gained a landlord (Hampson 1963: 129, 261).

Why does the ideology of privatisation persist, when it demonstrably undermines traditional forms of civil society? Chapter 1 noted how the competing discourses about the English enclosures have persisted into modern political debate. Franz von Benda-Beckmann (2001) argues that, because economic development in Europe and the United States has been based on individual property ownership, communal property can unjustly be represented as diagnostic of archaic and economically undeveloped societies. If, as was argued during the enclosures debate, ownership were freed from communal constraints this would allow land to be mortgaged against bank loans for investment in better methods of production. Innovative individuals would no longer be constrained by collective practices, and the wealthy could purchase land once it became a marketable commodity.

Joel Migdal documents how, despite claiming to follow Adam Smith's ideology of the 'invisible hand', colonial powers visibly intervened to ensure the market's penetration into subsistence production and local trade (1988: 56). Communal landholding was abolished in states from Mexico to the Ottoman Empire. Migdal argues that privatisation of land was firstly intended to secure the state's hegemonic rule, an argument complemented by Ester Kingston-Mann's (2003) account of Soviet hostility to the Russian *mir* or commune (see above, chapter 1). The second goal was to exploit the greatly increased demand in Europe and the United States for cotton, sugar, coffee, jute, indigo etc., benefiting elite landholders and potentially increasing the state's income from taxation, but at the cost of removing land from subsistence production.

Yet communal landholding is not necessarily irrational. Benda-Beckmann (2001) argues that the dominant function of lineage property among peasant cultivators is to provide the material basis for the continuity of the descent group and its future members. This imposes severe restrictions on permanent or temporary transfers to persons outside the group (Benda-Beckmann 2001: 307, cf. Benda-Beckmann 1990, cited in chapter 2). From the perspective of William Hamilton's theory of kin-selection, where people are confident their children will inherit rights to the land they have worked, responsible custodianship of the land becomes a way of increasing parents' 'inclusive fitness', that is, of ensuring their genes are transmitted through future generations. If privatised land falls into the hands of decision-makers such as state officials who do not themselves depend entirely on the resource and do not live in its environment, but *do* seek to maximise revenue from that resource, they are more likely to inflict degradation. 'The tragedy of the commons seems more a problem of *free raiders* than of free riders' (Benda-Beckmann 2001: 305). The market, combined with state redistribution of title to land, allows unrestrained access to natural resources and destroys the trust and confidence on which local civil society is based (Benda-Beckmann and Benda-Beckmann 1999: 39). The opportunity to gain individual ownership is an invitation to defect from long-term co-operation. Kojo Sebastian Amanor (1999) argues that, in Ghana, high costs and insecurity have caused many farmers to sign contracts with agribusinesses to produce specified crops in specified quantities. This gives some guarantee of prices, but prevents farmers seeking higher prices on the open market (cf. Rosenberg 1988: 163 on Nestlé's exploitation of dairy farming in the French Alps). Such contracts allow agribusiness to treat African farmers as employees without having to provide social security or welfare (Amanor 1999: 27–8), but they suffer a high level of free-riding, as crops are raided and illegally processed by women and young men who have been displaced from formal, legal areas of activity (Amanor 1999: 141).

In his study of the small Sudanese town of Maiurno, Mark Duffield (1981) shows how peasants and the local elite pursue different strategies. By rotating crops, peasant households can preserve the fertility of the soil for twenty to thirty years, before allowing it to return to fallow. Because they depend on the land for their subsistence it is in their interests to maintain its fertility. The rich, however, see farming primarily as a short-term means of raising cash to invest in commerce. The long-term fate of the land is not of interest to them because it is not their only form of capital. They treat land as a consumable resource and will reinvest their profits from cash crops in other activities such as transport or shop-keeping when the land is exhausted. The traditional peasantry of Maiurno is squeezed between local capitalists and a growing body of landless wage-labourers.

The discourse of enclosure has therefore continued because the goals remain the same. Enclosure 'worked' in England because the Industrial Revolution created more or less enough jobs to absorb the displaced rural population, and there was high demand for the staple agricultural products produced on enclosed land. Where agricultural markets are more volatile, and where cities offer insufficient employment, the risk of social unrest foreseen by critics of enclosure is higher. We witness the same strategy played out in diverse social environments.

The expansion of mechanised agriculture in northern Sudan prompted the state to appropriate nomads' grazing land for cultivation (Duffield 1994). Peasant producers benefited but nomads, including Baggara Arabs, suffered. By the 1980s, the process of 'asset transfer' had acquired a violent, sectarian and inter-ethnic character, which rekindled civil war between Arab and African Sudanese. The Baggara (Muslim Arabs), for example, turned on the Nilotic cattle-herding Dinka and Nuer whose land lies further south in their search for grazing land, asserting that Pagan/Christian Nilotes were not 'fit' to own such wealth in cattle. This made the Baggara 'ready tools in the government's strategy of arming irregular militias' (Duffield 1994: 54); a strategy currently (2005) directed against the Fur of the southwest Sudan.

Competition for natural resources

If the state is to benefit from privatisation, it must be sufficiently powerful to prevent rival groups capturing the profits. Since private property can be mortgaged and sold, increasingly powerful entrepreneurs can use privatisation to gain control of vast areas of land and organise the cultivation of export crops for personal profit. Success in breaking down local civil society can undermine the goal of securing undivided allegiance to the state. Privatisation of land in Latin America had allowed the appearance of a new class of landlords hostile to state centralisation, while formerly independent peasants were reduced to poverty as tenants. Far from abolishing haciendas, Mexican privatisation laws made it easier for big landlords to seize land that had not been properly registered. By 1910, less than 1 per cent of the families in Mexico owned 85 per cent of the land (Migdal 1988: 63). In Russia, privatisation was carried out during the early 1990s with little regard for its empowering effect upon criminal organisations who could afford to purchase state enterprises. The Russian 'mafiya' was not created by privatisation, but the shift in distribution of resources caused by privatisation made organised crime a more 'adaptive' strategy (see Handelman 1994).

Corporations form a crucial part of civil society in a capitalist market economy. Where the state lacks the means to collect taxes, that wealth can be appropriated to empower other social organisations. Duffield estimates that in Kenya and Russia only 40 per cent of the gross national product is gained through legal and publicly regulated activities; in Angola it may be no more than 10 per cent (Duffield 2001: 141). Even where trade of oil and timber is legal, multinational corporations increasingly protect their enclaves with corporate mercenaries, while illegal drug dealers are even more likely to resort to violence.

James Fairhead (2000) has written a hard-hitting paper on the war on the borders of Rwanda and the Congo. Following the same line as Duffield and Richards, he criticises the popular supposition that humanitarian crises are caused by local over-exploitation of the environment and ensuing poverty. International intervention can exacerbate local tensions by favouring one side, especially where access to vital minerals (cobalt, diamonds etc.) is the prize, and a secondary prize is control over the labour needed to exploit them. Richards similarly writes that 'the violence of the Sierra Leone conflict is . . . moored, culturally, in the hybrid Atlantic world of international commerce in which, over many years, Europeans and Americans have played a prominent and often violent part' (Richards 1996: xvii). Brian Ferguson (2003: 6) describes how 'extra-official products' such as diamonds and drugs enter international trade. Extra-governmental and often illegal organisations increase in wealth and power so as to undermine the state, while the state's revenue decreases (Ferguson 2003: 7).

The examples given above demonstrate repeatedly that Third World states live in an evolutionary economic environment that is shaped by the West. The Indian government was pushed to liberalise its economy by foreign investors who wanted access to India's cheap labour and its untapped consumer markets (Lessinger 2003: 169). Western economic policy influences social stability in the Third World, and the breakdown of civil society in such states cannot simply be attributed to their inherent anarchy. Rather, contemporary nation states are embedded in an economic fitness landscape where each state influences the stability of others and shapes the strategies of local groups who find themselves competing for resources. The groups exercising social control in civil society may be heterogeneous in form (family versus tribe), and in the rules they apply (personal loyalty versus profit maximization). The distribution of social control may be fragmented or concentrated. Weak states are threatened by strong organisations below the level of state, such as clans, ethnic and religious organisations – elements of civil society. Providing they have persisted as alternative strategies for social organisation, ethnicity, kinship and selective patronage are therefore likely to come to the fore where resources have declined to such an extent that the existing state structure is unsustainable. Such organisations may advocate competing rules for access to and management of resources. If these rules

are contested, violent conflict may break out. Reyna argues
that the distribution of force in a field depends on *how much*
and *what kind* of force is available to the groups participating. In a strong state, violent force is effectively confined to
government institutions; it is highly concentrated, and has low
dispersion. But force may be 'both dispersed and concentrated
into the institutions of civil society. This makes it possible
for these institutions to be downright uncivil' (Reyna 2003:
265). Apparently anarchic social strategies can be explained
as locally rational responses to changes in the economic environment that undermine the power of the nation state, or its
ability to satisfy citizens' needs.

VIOLENCE AND CATASTROPHIC CHANGE

Alternative strategies and complex systems

Chapter 2 argued that two or more alternative strategies for
organising access to, and the exploitation of resources may
co-exist in the same fitness landscape (Mormons in capitalist America, producer co-operatives and entrepreneurs in
Europe). The presence of alternative strategies does not necessarily cause social disorder. Violent disorder can be explained
through the concept of 'catastrophic' change, when a system moves rapidly from one state to another. Since politics is
underpinned by force, catastrophic change is often triggered
by a redistribution of the means to exercise force. Whether or
not violence results depends largely on whether the alternatives are mutually compatible or in conflict with one another.

In rural Hungary co-operatives and private family production were compatible, but this was no longer the case
when family enterprise was permitted in towns. Entrepreneurs
undermined, and eventually destroyed, the command

economy. The anthropologist Edmund Leach (1954) famously found that among the Kachin of highland northern Burma prior to the Second World War, some Kachin villages were autonomous and egalitarian, others under the authority of local Kachin chiefs. Historical evidence implied that particular villages had oscillated between the two forms. Ray Abrahams (1990) suggests the process identified by Leach in highland Burma could be accounted for by the theory of complex systems, whose behaviour is unpredictable and verges on the chaotic. Leach concluded that two ideal but conflicting forms of political organisation were recognised by the Kachin, the egalitarian *gumlao*, and the hierarchical *gumsa*. Valley princedoms were based on irrigated rice cultivation, while the Kachin living in the intervening highlands grew dry rice by means of swidden agriculture. Kachin crops provided less taxable surplus than irrigated rice and also obliged people to move every few years, giving them greater opportunities to travel beyond the boundaries of overbearing leaders, and rendering petty chiefship unstable. Leach argued that *gumsa* chiefs among the highland Kachin tended to accrue power until, seeking to emulate the princes of neighbouring valleys, they fell foul of contradictions in the use of highland resources, causing rebellious subjects to re-establish *gumlao* and regain autonomy over the control of their crops and women. Jack Goody (2001: 161–3) would interpret this as a case of civil society rebelling against the state. (David Nugent (1982) has argued that Kachin chiefs owed their power to the opium trade, and that the rebellions documented by Leach occurred when the British blocked opium trading.)

Fitness landscapes represent a type of complex system, described by Stuart Kauffman as 'order on the edge of chaos' (Kauffman 1993: 181). Abrahams drew a parallel between Leach's analysis and the archaeologist Colin Renfrew's explanation for the sudden origin of agriculture in western Asia about ten thousand years ago. Renfrew suggested catastrophe theory could explain the divergence of ways of life based on alternative subsistence strategies (in this case, foraging and cultivation). Under certain conditions, the costs and benefits for both may be equal, and a single community can follow a mixed economy, in this instance combining foraging with low-level husbandry. As conditions steadily change, their relative costs and benefits may shift. This occurred when the dual economy in socialist Hungary, combining private and co-operative production, was transferred to cities. Changing conditions may render alternatives such as foraging and cultivation incompatible *but equally satisfactory* solutions to the costs and benefits of subsistence. In the latter case, a bifurcation occurs in which some populations pursue a forager trajectory while others move into cultivation (Renfrew 1978: 207–10), or some pursue private enterprise while others join producer co-operatives or Mormon communities. If the two are incompatible, however, there may be a sudden ('catastrophic') abandonment of one strategy and a switch to exclusive dependence on the other (as is illustrated by the Kachin and by urban Hungary).

The same approach can be taken to analysis of violent social change in the twentieth century. The existing social order breaks down when competing strategies gain ascendancy. Ethnic and clan loyalties, for example, become more viable when trust in the state is undermined. If communities suspect that the state is favouring another sector of society, or if the state fails to provide physical protection, legal redress and a stable economy, people may suddenly reallocate their resources to support alternative leaders. As Migdal puts it, organisations such as states, ethnic groups, institutions based on social class, villages etc. offer individuals 'the components for survival strategies' (Migdal 1988: 29). These strategies are not 'primordial', in the sense of welling up from some original stratum of human society, but active, and of contemporary relevance. Political contests arise over which social strategies to implement.

A revolution is therefore a contest with an uncertain outcome (cf. Bailey 1969). Unstable social systems may provide people with realisable options; each pathway transforming the social system in different ways. When a complex system enters an unstable state, individual action can have a noticeable impact; this is the so-called 'butterfly effect', where the course of a storm can supposedly be altered by the fluttering of a butterfly's wings (see Stewart 1997 and Layton 2000: 358–9). The social order is vulnerable to partisan leaders who offer quick solutions to growing hardship.

Migdal explains the spread of the nation state as a kind of arms race, similar to the 'Red Queen' phenomenon in biological evolution that drives the spiralling co-evolution of predator and prey. New states come into being in response to existing states that are transforming the social environment. If existing states are to be resisted, then new ones must be created to counter them. Migdal argues that getting people to obey the rules of the state rather than those of the manor or clan was pursued less out of a desire for universal justice than with the aim of ensuring the state's leaders' survival by drawing power around them. There is, however, an implicit social contract, in the sense used by Hobbes and Rousseau, between the state and the people it governs. No state governs entirely by force. A government that fails to honour the social contract becomes vulnerable to other centres of power, in civil society.

The sudden abandonment of one strategy and a switch to exclusive dependence on another is exemplified by the overwhelming pressure for change that came from nationalist leaders as the Soviet Union disintegrated. As in the Yugoslavian federation, they rushed to gain assets and autonomy to assure

their position in the new regime. Popular demands for liber-
ties outside the Soviet system could be suppressed as long as
regional leaders received powerful support from the centre,
but not once the centre was weakened. Regional leaders and
their rivals now had strong incentives to recruit popular support by presenting themselves as authentic representatives of
the local people. As occurred during *gumlao* revolt in highland
Burma, a 'catastrophic' switch to a new, autonomous political
strategy took place. Douglas McAdam, Sidney Tarrow and
Charles Tilly (2001) argue that one of the most important vari-
ables in the trajectory of violent social change is the defection
of members of the armed forces from the ruling coalition,
while others have shown that large numbers of unemployed
young men can readily be recruited as armed supporters of
aspiring leaders.

Government as a resource

Ferguson (2003) is critical of the 'weak state' concept. He
points out that where poverty is pervasive even 'weak' governments may be relatively wealthy, making access to government the source of the conflict. This point, while not (in
my assessment) undermining the general concept of weak
states, is substantiated by a number of African case studies.
Where NGOs bypass the state, replacing the state's hierarchical structures with horizontal cross-national connections,
they also weaken the state. Where NGOs depend on existing
elites or state structures, however, they increase the resources
available to those in power. If the elite's hold on power is weak,
control of the state may be challenged by rivals.

Duffield (1994) argues the key to understanding the survival of the state in countries such as the Sudan is to recognise
that disasters have winners as well as losers. During the 1980s,
the Sudanese government captured large sums intended as

local aid by overvaluing its currency, and requiring office rents, salaries of national employees etc. to be paid in the local currency. In this way, Sudan gained a sum equivalent to half its annual military expenditure. Reyna (2003), however, argues that the civil wars fought in Chad since independence have been driven by competition for high office, for control of the state. Probably 80 per cent of Chadians are subsistence farmers. The only occupation that allows the accumulation of wealth is that of high government official. Such wealth was typically invested in local land and business, and in international business deals.

Günter Schlee (2002) reports a similar pattern in Somalia. During the United Nations' intervention in Somalia during the early 1990s the numerous UN officials living in a select quarter of Mogadishu earned on average forty-five times more than a Somali minister. As Schlee suggests, it is not surprising Somali bureaucrats made the food aid industry and other charitable institutions pay for allowing them to help the country. Aid agency representatives, keen to complete their project and move on to the next one, were often very willing to pay bribes. Goods disappeared, along with posts allocated to projects. Hence, as in the Sudan, 'the state rapidly turned into an instrument for accessing help from the outside and for creaming off external resources' (Schlee 2002: 256). While he controlled the port of Mogadishu, General Aideed was able to levy exorbitant taxes and take a direct cut of 10–20 per cent of the incoming food. It is therefore not surprising that rival groups challenged him for control of the Somali state.

Loose molecules

A revolutionary transition is likely to be triggered by a shift in the balance of power between proponents of alternative strategies. Robert Kaplan argued that social order in Africa is being undermined by young men flocking to cities 'like loose molecules in a very unstable social fluid, a fluid . . . on the verge of igniting' (Kaplan 1994: 46). Kaplan attributes their flight from the countryside to over-population, the spread of disease, deforestation and soil erosion; all in his opinion brought about by local mismanagement. Duffield (2001: 27) traces the origin of the approach advocated by Kaplan to a UN report published in 1981. The author, Sadruddin Aga Khan, attributed the global rise in refugees during the 1970s to the ready supply of arms to unstable governments, high population growth, unemployment, desertification and rapid urbanisation in the developing world. The counter view advocated by developing states, that political instability was caused by global inequality and balance of trade problems (i.e. underdevelopment), made less impact. Sadruddin Aga Khan's explanation was attractive because it shifted blame from the West to the victims of global change.

Richards (1996) challenges Kaplan's argument, which he terms the 'New Barbarism thesis'. The war in Sierra Leone grew out of the war in Liberia, the most sparsely populated and densely forested country in the region. The war in Liberia cannot therefore have been caused by land shortage. Sierra Leone is more densely populated and has suffered more deforestation, but Kaplan's data are erroneous (Richards 1996: 117–24). In Sierra Leone rural population densities are declining and there is under-used agricultural land. Richards contends the war in Sierra Leone was caused by political collapse and state recession, not overpopulation and land degradation (see above).

Nonetheless, young unemployed or under-employed men frequently figure in accounts of recent social disorder in Africa. Reyna (2003) reports that many of the soldiers powering the civil wars in Chad are young men who have some schooling, but have been unable to complete secondary school. Many dream of becoming government officials, but in practice join the urban unemployed, or return to rural villages. Many of the Hutu extremist militias in Rwanda were also unemployed or under-employed adolescent males armed only with clubs and machetes (Taylor 1999: 5). Rwanda is the most densely populated country in sub-Saharan Africa. Christopher Taylor concedes that lack of land contributed to the genocide, but the land is fertile and intensively cultivated, and two acres can support a family of nine. However, coffee is virtually the only export. Drought, combined with the decrease in world coffee prices and a World Bank structural adjustment programme, caused thousands in southwestern Rwanda to flee to neighbouring countries. Young unemployed or under-employed men could find work by participating in the genocide. 'Just by becoming an *Interahamwe* and executing Tutsi, one could elevate oneself to the status of "state employee". One could even expect eventual compensation from the state for one's services and indeed this was sometimes given and much more frequently promised' (Taylor 1999: 141).

Nor are 'loose molecules' only found in Africa. Johanna Lessinger notes that modernising capitalist development often tends, if incomplete, to produce large numbers of semi-educated, under-employed young men. In India, the Hindu Nationalist Party, the VHP, 'has now added a youth wing to tap the frustrations of young, unemployed urban men who enjoy marching about, armed with spears' (Lessinger 2003: 162). Bette Denich describes how, during the months before war in the Balkans, 'A panoply of previously banned flags, songs, insignia and uniforms provided a made-to-order "anti-hero" image, massively attracting the same young people who had found themselves "superfluous" during the years of economic crisis' (Denich 2003: 192). A former Bosnian Serb camp guard told Denich that many people under twenty-five had never had a job. Once Muslim and Serb nationalists offered them a hundred marks, they could then do what they liked with them.

The 'loose molecules' metaphor stands for a real phenomenon, but socially volatile young men are not produced by some anarchy inherent in society; they are a product of the global economy.

Game theory, and the Prisoner's Dilemma

Is it possible to quantify the point at which a catastrophic shift between incompatible strategies will occur? Chapter 2 discussed two ways of analysing the breakdown of mutual trust. Axelrod's (1990) experiments with the Prisoner's Dilemma demonstrated that, for reciprocity to persist, people must not only have experience of each other as trustworthy partners in previous social exchanges, but must also anticipate that they will remain dependent on one another indefinitely. Axelrod discovered that, if partners in mutual aid know they are participating for the last time, and will not depend on each other for further co-operation, they will have no incentive to give their time and resources to help others and will withdraw into selfishness (Axelrod 1990: 10–13). McAdam, Tarrow and Tilly (2001: 251) describe the situation in Russia under Gorbachev's reforms in these terms: 'Time horizons contracted rapidly. On the large scale and the small, people could no longer count on payoffs from long-term investment in the existing system; they reoriented to short-term gains and exit strategies.' Like the two prisoners caught in the dilemma, they switched to mutual defection. Stef Jansen analyses the published accounts of three women (two Croat, one Serb) of the dissolution of the Yugoslavian state. One (Dubravka Ugrešic) wrote, 'suddenly everything had to change: address books, the language and our names, our identity . . . Everything changed with astonishing speed into old garbage' (Jansen 1998: 95). People who had not discarded their Yugoslav identities became known as 'Yugozombies'.

The breakdown of mutual trust can also be interpreted as the consequence of moving from a non-zero-sum game to a zero-sum game. If everyone's wellbeing can be enhanced by co-operation, they have a strong motive to work together (a non-zero sum game). If resources are perceived to be fixed, then conflict will break out in the scramble to secure the largest portion for oneself. Ethnicity and kinship provide appropriate organisations within civil society through which to realise that goal. Schlee (2004) analyses the dynamics of the coalitions that strove to control government during the civil war in Somalia in these terms.

Terrorism is an effective way of eroding trust in the social order. Renos Papadopoulos (2002) describes his therapeutic work at the Tavistock Clinic, with Bosnian ex-camp prisoners freed by the Red Cross. He records that survivors of atrocities not only lose their identifiable material possessions and human relationships; they also lose the reality of belonging to a language group, and to a geographical and built landscape. When neighbours attack each other, the victims lose even their personal identity and the ability to trust in social relationships. Alfred Garwood draws on his own experiences as a child survivor of the Holocaust, arguing that Nazi behaviour toward enforced ghettos and concentration camps was designed to make the Jews feel inadequate. 'In Germany and Austria increasingly anti-Jewish laws and public humiliation were intended to disempower, impoverish and terrorise . . . In the camps, infantilisation, humiliation, starvation, torture and murder were the daily fare' (Garwood

2002: 363). The anthropologist Claude Lévi-Strauss's autobi-
ographical *Tristes tropiques* contains a moving account of the
motley collection of passengers on a ship escaping Europe
at the start of the Second World War. Many were severely
affected by the spitefulness and stupidity they had encountered from the crew, who knew the refugees had been stripped
of their social identity to become nonentities (Lévi-Strauss
1973: 29).

In India, Hindu extremist violence was intended to paralyse
the existing state apparatus by creating chaos, terror and breakdown of community, until particular localities were ungovern-
able. This is 'a serious threat in a country with an enormous,
impoverished population and a poorly funded, rather fragile
state mechanism' (Lessinger 2003: 172). Richards challenges
Kaplan's attribution of violence in recent African civil wars
to irrational religious beliefs. Richards responds that while
it may be indefensible, terror is not irrational; it is supposed to unsettle its victims. Terror tactics aim to demor-
alise better-armed soldiers and control villagers (Richards
1996: xx). Women's hands were cut off in Sierra Leone to prevent them harvesting crops. With no harvest accessible, young
recruits had no incentive to desert the rebels and return to their
villages.

Unlike ordinary criminals, terrorists aim to provoke an
over-reaction by the state. 'If it began to appear to the civilian
populations that the liberal democratic nature of the society
was being damaged by the reaction of the government, then
the authorities would be blamed for the loss of freedom in the
long-term, not the terrorists' (Alderdice 2002: 9). Terrorist
organisations regularly claim responsibility for their actions.
Such organisations aim to violate social norms and hence
provoke outrage, so that they cannot be ignored. Terrorists
aim to destroy faith in others' willingness to reciprocate, and
hence to confront people with the lack of trust that leads to

mutual defection in the Prisoner's Dilemma, and retreat into the security of one's own ethnic or kin group.

STRATEGIES FOR REDRAWING THE LIMITS OF CIVIL SOCIETY: (1) KINSHIP

Chapter 1 argued that kinship is not a 'primordial' basis for social relationships, but a rational way of sustaining social organisation. In his classic anthropological analysis of the cattle-herding Nuer of the southern Sudan, Edward Evans-Pritchard (1940) showed how a politically uncentralised society can sustain social order. Evans-Pritchard argued that the unity of each Nuer 'tribe' had an ecological basis: each tribe united to defend grazing and water for livestock. As Dyson-Hudson and Smith later clarified (1978), pasture and water are too sparse and unpredictable to justify smaller social groups defending particular patches. In Evans-Pritchard's time, the Nuer had no chiefs, but within the tribe Nuer recognised mediators who could intervene to resolve feuds, because everyone shared a joint interest in guaranteeing freedom of movement. Cattle were, on the other hand, owned by lineages (groups reputedly descended from a common male ancestor) within the tribe. Households managed their own herds but could borrow cattle from others in their own lineage if they lost livestock through raiding, disease or drought. The lineage provided mutual insurance for its members (cf. Spencer 1965 on the related Samburu). Disputes were therefore most likely to break out between different lineages in the same tribe. Marriage took place between lineages within the tribe, creating alliances between households.

In Northern Albania and Somalia, the traditional social organisation of peasant farmers and herders was also based on autonomous lineages, linked by marriage alliances or opposed through feuding. The anthropologists who described these cases noted that both societies resembled the Nuer. In the absence of a reliable state organisation, local allegiances were important. The breakdown of the state resulted in the resurgence of lineage organisation as a more effective strategy for ensuring personal survival. Lineage organisation persisted because it continued to meet local social needs and was even supported by weak state government as a means of indirectly extending government power to the local level.

Somalia

Prior to European colonisation there was no centralised state in Somalia. Somalis belonged to autonomous lineages and were only united by a common language (Lewis 1997: 181). Somalia is the sole country in Africa where the majority still practise nomadic pastoralism. Pastoral politics is based on coalitions of kin, as among the Nuer. Larger groups have an advantage in disputes, because their strength discourages smaller groups from taking vengeance, and each member has to contribute less when compensation for murder is paid. Schlee (2002) argues that force underlies rather than bends the rules.

Somalia was colonised after the opening of the Suez Canal in 1869 but became an independent nation state in 1960. After independence, the state fell apart. The erroneous notion that pastoralism is backward and unproductive, held by both the Somali state and external development agencies, led to increasing neglect of the pastoral economy. Lack of alternative exports limited the income available to the state. Civil servants were paid the same rate throughout the 1960s, despite hyperinflation.

In response to the bankruptcy of the state, General Mohamad Siad Barre staged a successful coup in 1969. His own clan provided the core of his power base, supported by his mother's clan. His son-in-law's clan controlled the national security service (Lewis 1997: 183n). Lineage organisation had taken control of the state. Siad Barre assumed sole right to allocate rights to land and water, eradicating customary tenure and therefore the authority of local leaders. But Siad Barre undermined his own attempts to eliminate the power base of clans by also using the clan system to his own advantage. He pitted clan against clan, sub-clan against sub-clan, in order to maximise his power. His 'distribution of rewards and punishments was carefully calculated to ensure a network of loyal supporters spread throughout all clans' (Besteman 2003: 292).

In 1977 Barre launched a failed attack on the Ogaden region of southern Ethiopia, peopled by clans related to the Somalis. Barre's defeat in Ethiopia weakened his army. Clans in the north of Somalia rebelled against his rule. Human rights organisations eventually persuaded foreign governments to stop providing aid. Barre's reach dwindled to members of his own clan, the Marehan. Even parts of his mother's clan and son-in-law's clan defected (Schlee 2002: 257). Siad Barre was overthrown in 1991 by the Hawiye group of clans, led by General Aideed. The north reacted by declaring itself independent within the borders of Somaliland, the former British colony (Lewis 1997: 184). Ioan Lewis cited the experience of a Somali friend, a former Minister of the Interior, who decided to return to his clan in the north. He and a group of friends and relatives formed a convoy of seventy vehicles, which took two months to complete a journey that in peacetime would have taken twenty-four hours. The convoy had its own armed escorts, and was forced to hire local guides and protectors for each of the clan territories they crossed. Four vehicles were looted, one by its armed escort. Eighteen people died on the journey and thirty were injured, but nine babies were born.

In the remainder of Somalia, leaders of rival clans continued to battle for power. By 1990 there were no courts and no
university: academics and lawyers were out of work (Bowden
1999: 114). In the four months between November 1991 and
February 1992, it is estimated that 14,000 people were killed.
Each side attacked the agricultural region between the two
southern rivers that provides much of Somalia's food. Approximately 11,000 southerners fled to Kenya and other countries
(Declich 2001). With farming devastated, famine spread and
30,000 more died from starvation.

Schlee argues that Somali lineage society is not immutable,
but Somali warlords must nonetheless follow cultural patterns
when they build up alliances. As Giddens (1984: 170) pointed
out, social structures are both enabling and constraining. 'The
clan organisation provides them with the tools and the material
of military recruitment while, at the same time, it limits their
freedom of choice in recruiting who they want' (Schlee 2004:
151). Opting for a particular rhetoric, such as brotherhood with
another Somali group, forecloses the possibility of marriage
with that group. The logic of alliance may also mean that one's
brother's brothers also demand hospitality. One may become
entangled in more relationships than one can oversee oneself,
while some people's decisions about which identity to adopt
affect others who were left out of that decision.

Albania

Albania is inhabited by two major ethnic groups, the Ghegs in
the north, the Tosks in the south. Ian Whitaker describes the
Ghegs as 'the only true example of a tribal system surviving in
Europe until the mid-twentieth century' (Whitaker 1968: 254).
The clan (*fis*) was a group of people claiming descent from a
common male ancestor over fourteen to fifteen generations,

although many links may be fictitious. The living members of the lineage consisted of a number of extended family households, some containing as many as sixty to ninety people, who owned property in common (Whitaker 1968: 256). A traditional 'territory' in northern Albania contained a conquering clan, previous inhabitants and newer arrivals (Doja 1999).

The traditional Albanian law code of *kanun* insists, among other things, upon absolute loyalty to one's kin group and hence encourages treachery toward others. Adherence to *kanun* promotes feuding (Boehm 1992), but also provides procedures for ending a feud. 'People are divided into friend and foe through employing "tradition" as a moral code that justifies categories of inclusion and exclusion' (Schwandner-Sievers 1999: 135). Blood feuds are brought to an end by creating classificatory brotherhood between the groups. Both parties must agree that honour has been satisfied (138). Clan leaders (*bajraktars*) acted as judges, who arbitrated in disputes. The Ottoman Turks, unable to reach individuals except through the mediating structures of civil society, relied on them heavily (Whitaker 1968: 259).

After the Second World War, the Communist Party made a point of attacking what it called the 'traditional patriarchal family'. Powerful families were the most subject to persecution, poverty and humiliation (Schwandner-Sievers 1999: 148). Stephanie Schwandner-Sievers argues the communist state's weak hold over local communities nonetheless led it covertly to continue to rely upon traditional local leaders (1999: 135; cf. Zubaida 2001: 243 on the Middle East). She also writes, 'The concepts of honour and humiliation, of alternating appeasement and violence, were reproduced by the ideology and actions of the highest communist officials' (136). The collapse of communism created a 'law vacuum', causing a reversion to earlier social procedures, not because they were primordial but because the procedures had tacitly been allowed to continue. *Kanun* was revived and, perhaps, reinterpreted after the socialist government collapsed. Traditionally powerful families set out to recover their status, and reverse the socialist redistribution of land. Because they had not joined the Communist Party, the honour of traditionally powerful families was uncompromised (139).

The status of a family now again depends on its ability to defend itself and kill others. Violent interactions are driven by a family's estimation of its own status and integrity, the aim to be respected by others, and actual village opinion. 'People . . . want to legitimize political violence and killing and to claim self-regulation and the monopoly of violence in opposition to the State' (Schwandner-Sievers 1999: 134). High status families once again guarantee the safety of others, their clients. The protected family accepts a lower status.

STRATEGIES FOR REDRAWING THE LIMITS OF
CIVIL SOCIETY: (II) ETHNICITY

Seligman (1992) and Gellner (1994) regarded ethnicity and kinship as two irredeemably 'primordial' and irrational types of social allegiance that undermined modern civil society. Chapter 1 argued this view arises from a particular vision of civil society as something that crystallised at a particular point in 'human progress'; something associated with a market economy, in which civil society should support the state if the state allows free trade and private property, but oppose it if the state is antagonistic to these traits. Chapter 1 went on to argue for a broader definition of civil society, and criticised the supposition that social behaviour associated with Western society since the eighteenth century is unique in its rationality.

Like kinship, ethnicity is flexible. Fredrik Barth, who introduced use of game theory to anthropology (Barth 1959), also transformed anthropologists' understanding of ethnic identity. Barth (1969) argued against the primordial character of ethnicity. He noted that people can join or leave ethnic groups, and ethnic groups are often interdependent rather than isolates, defined in opposition to each other. Barth characteristically advocated a generative approach to ethnicity, asking why participants found ethnic identity useful in social interaction and why, therefore, ethnic boundaries persisted. He argued that sharing a common culture is a result, rather than a cause, of individuals' decisions. Case studies showed that some cultural features are used by actors as signals of identity and difference, while other potential markers are ignored, demonstrating that strategic decisions are being made. Identifying someone else as a member of one's ethnic group implies an assumption that 'the two are fundamentally "playing the same game"' (Barth 1969: 15), while treating the other as a stranger from another ethnic group assumes fewer shared understandings and different value judgements. Barth advocated treating each ethnic group as part of other such groups' environment, leading to separation, interdependence or competition. People will join, and identify with, an ethnic group if they need to do so to obtain essential resources.[1]

If ethnic identity is only one option, yet is advocated as the most reliable source of mutual aid, what gives ethnic history contemporary salience (Turton 1997: 11)? 'Constructed, manipulated histories must be true enough to the known past, and responsive enough to present anxieties, to be believable' (Ferguson 2003: 21). During conflict between ethnic groups, opposing sides often start and stop history at different points, often starting where their ancestors were victims of unjustified

---

[1] Song (2003) points out that movement between ethnic groups is more difficult where ethnicity is associated with physical difference.

aggression. Intellectuals can thus play a crucial role in retelling history so as to justify ethnic exclusiveness and the persecution of less powerful communities. Eric Hobsbawm wrote that 'historians are to nationalists what poppy-growers in Pakistan are to heroin addicts' (Hobsbawm 1992: 3, cited in Turton 1997: 14). This point is reiterated by Gallagher (1997: 59), writing on Yugoslavia. The role of intellectuals and mass media in promoting the Rwandan genocide is a pervasive theme in Taylor's account (Taylor 1999, particularly 55–8). Like the campaigns against immigration mounted by the tabloid press in the United Kingdom, mass media can promote discourses that legitimate subversive strategies at moments of potentially catastrophic change. Local perceptions may not be realistic, but unscrupulous political leaders may argue unfairly for their constituency. Hindu nationalists disregard the fact that Indian Muslims are generally poorer than Hindus, less polygamous, own less land, have a lower life expectancy and higher unemployment, and instead allege that Muslims have an unfair advantage in competition for apparently limited resources (Rao and Reddy 2001). They advocate, in other words, a view of inter-ethnic relations as a zero-sum game. Nandini Rao and C. Rammanohar Reddy (2001) look at the role of the media in shaping the discourse of Hindu nationalism. Marcus Banks (1999) analyses the way that Western mass media provided outsiders with over-simplified understandings of the Bosnian conflict, legitimising claims for ethnic identity.

The following paragraphs look at the role of ethnic allegiance in the breakdown of social order in Indonesia, northern India and Yugoslavia, arguing that ethnic identity is not primordial but is used strategically to promote competition for resources, when these are perceived to be fixed, and to break down the trust upon which wider social networks of co-operation and reciprocity depend. The aim is not to determine whether or not civil society is a 'good thing', merely to explain why people behave in certain ways – why they adopt particular social strategies – in certain circumstances; to examine, in other words, which familiar strategies in the actor's habitus best advance his or her interests in the local social and economic environment.

Indonesia

Keebet von Benda-Beckmann's study (2004) of recent violence on the Indonesian island of Ambon illustrates the situational relevance of ethnic identity, and the historical contingency of its construction. The violence began on 19 January 1999, when an Ambonese motor taxi driver got into a fight with a Buginese tricycle taxi rider. While this type of fight had often occurred before in the multi-ethnic neighbourhood, such fights were usually transient. This time, however, the fight led to a long period of rioting that has approached civil war. Christian and Muslim religious leaders, local leaders, influential intellectuals, high politicians and even the president tried to create peace and reconciliation, but in vain. Why had society reached a critical point, where catastrophic social change was possible?

Christianity and Islam were both introduced to the region in the late sixteenth and early seventeenth centuries, during a time of colonial competition between Dutch and Portuguese. Those who supported the Dutch adopted Christianity, while those who supported Moluccan leaders and the Portuguese adopted Islam. Further fault lines were introduced during the colonial period, when the Dutch halted development of the inter-village political structures that were the first steps toward indigenous state formation. *Adat* (traditional law) can therefore now only be used to resolve disputes within, not between, villages. During the nineteenth century Butonese migrants were encouraged to settle between existing villages, to act as a buffer zone between competing parties. The Dutch favoured Christians, creating a Christian state administrative system. This caused a very biased pattern of access to higher education until a campaign was launched during the 1980s for the appointment of Muslim officials in provincial administration. While the admission of Muslims increased the sense of insecurity among Christians, Christians and Muslims are united against Butonese immigrants in defending the principle that only native ethnic Ambonese are eligible for appointment. Contemporary ethnicity in Indonesia is therefore far from 'primeval'; it has repeatedly been reconstructed and given contemporary salience by colonial and post-colonial government policies.

The region had attempted to achieve independence from Indonesia immediately after the colonial period. In response, the Indonesian government turned Ambon into an important naval base. Indonesia's ruler Suharto granted one of his sons a monopoly on the lucrative trade in cloves and ownership of one of the largest factories locally producing clove cigarettes. One of the greatest problems for the state is therefore the failure of the implicit social contract between people and government.

Benda-Beckmann argues that although the taxi driver was Christian and the becak (tricycle taxi) driver Muslim, religion was at first only marginally significant. The dispute was between a local population and a population of recent migrants, and was concerned with access to jobs in the private economy. Becak driving had until then been dominated by immigrant Buginese and Macassarese. Suffering from the effects of the economic depression, local Ambonese tried to break down this ethnic segmentation and move into pedal-powered taxi operation. Ethnic identity was more significant than the Christian/Muslim divide. Soon, however, disloyal high officers were reported to be using semi-militia and groups of militant youths to provoke unrest and hence enhance their position. The police were reported to side with Christians and the army with Muslims, while the navy appears to have remained neutral. As in Paris during the 1790 revolution, the state was losing its monopoly over the control of force.

India

Violence is not inevitable or primordial in India. Hindus and Muslims have lived together peacefully, even fruitfully, for long periods. Rao and Reddy (2001) explain the Hindu Nationalist Party's campaign to demolish the mosque at Ayodhya that provided one of the starting points for the present study as an opportunist exploitation of the ruling Congress Party's weakness during the early 1990s. The Congress Party was in decline, but none of the competing parties was powerful enough to replace it. The Congress government was bound to defend India's secular constitution but, in opposing the destruction of the mosque, it could be made to appear to support the Muslim minority against the Hindu majority.

Lessinger (2003) argues that religion is an effective means of mobilising violence in India because religious communities are not localised. Muslims and Christians can be constructed as ubiquitous enemies of Hinduism, and Hinduism identified with Indian nationalism. McAdam, Tarrow and Tilly (2001), drawing on the anthropological work of Beth Roy, similarly argue that religion is not necessarily an effective way of defining factions at the village level. However, the higher a local dispute goes the more it can be redefined as a dispute between Muslims and Hindus, not one between neighbours. Caste is locally relevant but ineffective as an organising principle for political dispute at the national level because castes are too diverse. Religion provides a simpler, more pervasive set of oppositions. As Fredrik Barth predicted, during any dispute a particular subset of identities emerges as their political potential in the current conflict becomes apparent. Thus, during the violence that followed the destruction of the mosque at Ayodhya by Hindu extremists, a killing in Hyderabad was highlighted at the time as the Hindu murder of a Muslim, although it later proved actually to be linked to a dispute between two local gangs over land.

Former Yugoslavia

After the Yugoslav Communist Party was disbanded in January 1990, nationalism came to the fore. Serbs recalled the wartime atrocities of the Ustashe, pointing to the fact that Tudjman, the Croatian leader, had revived the chequer-board Croatian flag last flown by the Second World War Fascist Ustashe. Croatians countered by recalling massacres and forced relocations of Croats perpetrated by the wartime Serb Chetniks, and the killing of tens of thousands of anti-communist refugees turned back at the Austrian border by the British army (Denich 1994: 379, Tanner 1997: 160). As Denich writes, 'Conflicts over various issues in shifting localities were symbolically manipulated to polarize public opinion along the lines of resurgent ethnic identities.' Nationalists seized upon 'the random constellations that create opportunities for those who lurk off-stage with alternate scripts' (Denich 1994: 369). Taylor describes a similar process in Rwanda (Taylor 1999: 86).

As Yugoslavian unity broke down, however, many found it increasingly expedient not only to secure a new national identity, but to increase that nation's share of the limited area of land within former Yugoslavia's borders. Chasing people off land they had occupied for centuries was a particular problem in Bosnia, where Serbs made up nearly three-fourths of the farmers but only a third of the total population (Verderey 1999: 102). 'If the state was to be redefined, average citizens needed to redefine their way of accessing it and had reason to fear being "left out in the cold" in the prospective power allocation along ethnic lines' (Denich 2003: 191). During the Serb invasion of Croatia, Catholic churches were burnt down, birth and death registers destroyed and local museums ransacked, in attempts to destroy evidence of long-term Croatian residence. Denich quotes a Croatian Serb:

So long as Yugoslavia's federal structure was emphasized, we didn't raise questions about national [Serb or Croatian] consciousness and national institutions. We considered Yugoslavia to be our state . . . But now that there are fewer and fewer Yugoslavs and more and more Croats, Slovenians, Serbs, Albanians and so on, we realized that we Serbs in Croatia need to return to our own national identity. (Denich 1994: 377)

Other authors describe the same experience. Jansen has already been cited. Edward Vulliamy quotes a Bosnian who told him:

I never thought of myself as a Muslim. I don't know how to pray. I never went to a mosque. I'm European like you. I don't want the Arab world to help us; I want Europe to help us. But now I have to think of myself as a Muslim, not in a religious way, but as a member of a people. Now we are faced with obliteration, I have to understand what it is about me and my people they wish to obliterate. (Vulliamy 1994: 65, quoted in Gallagher 1997: 63)

CONCLUSION

The existing social order breaks down when changes in the economic and social 'fitness landscape' undermine the effectiveness of previously dominant social organisations and empower other, competing strategies. Civil institutions in the existing cultural repertoire may be promoted in place of the state, and may be used in novel ways. Transformation of the shape of the fitness landscape renders previously dominant strategies and institutions less adaptive than their alternatives, in the sense that they are no longer most effective at advancing the individual's survival.

Like Bourdieu and Giddens, Schlee argues that game theory must be combined with sociological analysis to understand why particular social identities are selected to promote conflict or alliance. Game theory is 'culture free', but in practice 'social identities cannot be made up at will, because they have to be plausible to others' (Schlee 2004: 137). Schlee, too, aims to strike a balance between the economic approach of game theory, in which individuals are considered separately to calculate the costs and benefits of engaging in conflict, and the sociological approach that focuses on social structures and their cognitive representations. Identities such as ethnic groups and nations are not, as Eric Hobsbawm and Terrence Ranger (1983) argued, 'inventions', but constructions built upon local materials and having an internal logic or coherence. Recent constructions may use old materials. Lévi-Strauss (1966) called this intellectual restructuring of existing cultural themes *bricolage*. *Bricolage* gives new social constructions familiarity, plausibility and a seeming naturalness. Applying this approach to the recent conflict in Somalia, Schlee argues that ethnicity and clanship are not immutable, but nor are warlords completely free to reorganise society.

They must follow cultural patterns when they construct new alliances. Giddens (1984: 170) pointed out that social structures are both enabling and constraining. As far as Somali warlords are concerned, 'The clan organisation provides them with the tools and the material of military recruitment while, at the same time, it limits their freedom of choice in recruiting who they want' (Schlee 2004: 151).

David Turton follows Glazier and Moynihan (1979), arguing that where the state holds finite resources (a zero-sum game) the best strategy is to make claims as a group which is small enough for its members to make significant gains. Ethnicity satisfies this need better than class. Ethnic identities can rapidly come and go but history can be selectively called upon to give them plausibility. Both ethnicity and kinship are cultural constructs whose salience depends on their political usefulness. When current conditions are unstable, people are vulnerable to claims by aspiring leaders that those currently in power cannot protect them, and that they would do better to fall back on local networks based on kinship, clientage or sect (Ferguson 2003: 29).

Since ethnicity and kinship both depend on exclusion, they are likely to precipitate violence. The trick performed by ethnic or nationalist extremists is to convince members of a multi-ethnic community that they can dispense with each other's help in future (the Prisoner's Dilemma) and instead fight for the largest share of limited resources by claiming an inalienable entitlement (a zero-sum game). Inter-ethnic violence is often started by small groups of armed men, but the terror they generate encourages a single axis of identity that overrides the previous complex of cross-cutting ties. Actors lose trust in those on whom they previously relied in a wider social network. The evolutionary landscape is transformed. Civil society provides alternative social groupings, which can compete for dominance in the state or withdraw into autarky, as society bifurcates along different trajectories.

In recent decades, the breakdown of social order is often precipitated by international economic intervention that diverts state income into repaying Western debts, or reduces the value of a country's principal exports. Privatisation of land may destroy the traditional civil society of rural communities and lineages, creating 'loose molecules', while the unsustainable cost of bureaucratic government can cause a return to patronage. The structure of the state, and the presence of complementary or competing social organisations in civil society, determine the course of social change once the existing social order gives way. The adoption of new strategies may have unforeseen consequences. Competing social strategies for control of resources may complement or conflict with one another, while the presence of agents of violence in the armed forces or unemployed young men can erode trust in the existing order and compel the adoption of strategies of exclusion. Ethnicity and kinship may capture people's trust and loyalty when the state can no longer be relied upon.

The West is profoundly implicated in the breakdown of social order in Africa. Our refusal to acknowledge that role is symptomatic of continuing Western racism. Robert Kaplan (1994) attributes African disorder entirely to indigenous causes: animist beliefs based on irrational spirit power, loose family structures responsible for high birth rates and the rapid spread of HIV and other diseases, reliance on the 'artificially' high price of cocoa and so forth. Kaplan's 'New Barbarism' carefully diverts attention away from the slavers and ivory traders of colonial times and their modern equivalents, the diamond smugglers, drug pushers and arms dealers who are implicated in the contemporary breakdown of order (Richards 1996: 87). The centre of the world economic system sucks resources out of the periphery to sustain its democratic, bureaucratic social system. As one moves outward to the periphery, a point is passed beyond which there are insufficient resources in local circulation to sustain democracy or bureaucracy, and patronage takes over. The transition may be sudden, catastrophic. It may be violent, but the changing environment that renders innovative strategies effective is not shaped by local agents alone.

CHAPTER 4

Warfare, biology and culture

As chapter 3 has shown, there have been many violent conflicts in Europe, Africa and Asia during the 1990s. Society seems increasingly vulnerable to apparently mindless acts of destruction. Some authors have concluded that humans are genetically disposed to violence and that culture provides an inadequate safeguard. Robert Kaplan argues that where there is mass poverty, people find liberation in violence. 'Only when people attain a certain economic, educational and cultural standard is this trait tranquilized' (Kaplan 1994: 73). Richard Wrangham and Dale Peterson argue there is evidence to suggest 'that chimpanzee-like violence preceded and paved the way for human war, making modern humans the dazed survivors of a continuous, 5-million-year habit of lethal aggression' (1996: 63). Chapter 4 therefore looks at evidence for the evolutionary significance of human warfare. It argues that warfare and peacemaking are equally important in human social evolution.

WAR IN SMALL-SCALE SOCIETIES

Paul Sillitoe defines war as 'a relationship of mutual hostility between two groups where both try by armed force to secure some gain at the other's expense' (Sillitoe 1978: 252; cf. Ember and Ember 1997: 3). The frequency of warfare among human populations has led some to argue that warfare is the product of an inherent human disposition, a genetically determined drive to aggression. During the 1960s, writers such as Robert Ardrey (1967) and Konrad Lorenz (1966 [1963]) popularised the idea that warfare was linked to 'instinctive' defence of territories, and therefore part of human nature. Raymond Dart's alleged evidence for cannibalism among Australopithecines (Dart 1925, 1959) appeared to confirm our ancestors had long killed members of their own species. Close parallels were drawn between human territoriality and that of other species. It has, however, since been shown that Australopithecines were victims of animal predators rather than members of their own species (Brain 1981). Research into territorial behaviour among animals reveals that territoriality is much more flexible than Lorenz and others had supposed. Even among bird species, aggressive behaviour and territoriality were found to depend on the specific costs and benefits of defending a resource in a particular environment. Davies, for example, studied the feeding patterns of pied wagtails in the Thames Valley of southern England and found that some individuals defended territories along a river, while others fed peacefully together in flocks on nearby flooded pools (Davies 1981).

More recent observations of inter-group violence and the defence of territories among chimpanzees have nonetheless again raised the prospect that warfare may be a genetic trait that we and chimpanzees have inherited from our common ancestors. Jane Goodall (1986) and Toshisada Nishida, Mariko Haraiwa-Hasegawa and Yukio Takahata (1985) reported cases of chimpanzees extending their territories by attack on adjacent groups, leading to the claim of a direct connection between male chimpanzee aggression and human warfare. A second observation has led to the claim that warfare evolved as a means of obtaining more wives. In many primate species, males typically leave their natal group at puberty and have to join another before they can reproduce. Among both chimpanzees and many small-scale human societies it is, on the contrary, females who leave their natal group to join their husband's group. Social anthropologists have long argued that the exchange of marriage partners between social groups is one of the most fundamental ways in which humans create alliances (Tylor 1903, Lévi-Strauss 1969). The discovery that females also move between groups among chimpanzees potentially throws light on the origin of the inter-group alliances in human society (Rodseth et al. 1991) and provides grounds for contending other groups were attacked to obtain their women rather than their territory. Napoleon Chagnon, for example, claims that Yanomami fight for access to women and to revenge deaths caused by sorcery (Chagnon 1997: 97).

Chimpanzees and humans are unusual if not, as Wrangham and Peterson claim, exceptional among animal species in killing members of their own species. 'That chimpanzees and humans kill members of neighbouring groups of their own species is, we have seen, a startling exception to the normal rule for animals' (Wrangham and Peterson 1996: 63). Claims of a common origin for human and chimpanzee inter-group aggression were stimulated by reports of so-called 'warfare' between two troops of chimpanzees at Gombe (Goodall 1986) and in the Mahale mountains, both sites in Tanzania (Nishida, Haraiwa-Hasegawa and Takahata 1985, Nishida 1979). Males appear to patrol territorial borders, and five attacks leading to deaths were observed at Gombe, culminating in the annexation of territory containing females.

There is still some question about how typical this pattern is, and to what extent it may have been influenced by the research team's practice of supplying the Gombe chimpanzees with bananas. After the supply of bananas had been drastically reduced, the Gombe community split into two groups and became polarised within a range they had previously apparently shared. Over a period of two years the males of the larger group killed at least some of those in the smaller group (Goodall 1986: 503–14). Encroaching farmers may also have displaced other chimpanzees into the area, increasing the pressure on food resources (Ghiglieri 1984: 8). It is plausible that provisioning and consequent population increase, followed by a sudden reduction in the food supply, affected the intensity and/or frequency of inter-group violence at Gombe. The Mahale mountains of Tanzania, on the eastern side of Lake Tanganyika, contain at least eight chimpanzee communities, each consisting of up to 100 individuals (Nishida, Takasaki and Takahata 1990: 66, table 3.2). While territories are generally exclusive, groups 'M' and 'N' showed, for a time, some overlap of ranges (Nishida, Takasaki and Takahata 1990: 71, fig. 3.4). Group 'M' subsequently gained exclusive access to the area previously shared. There is circumstantial evidence for raiding, but no direct evidence that one group of males systematically wiped out another in order to gain access to females. As Joseph Manson and Richard Wrangham (1991) therefore acknowledge, there are only two known cases (one confirmed and one probable) of group extinction via lethal raiding (Manson and Wrangham 1991: 371).[1]

---

[1] Michael Wilson, William Wallauer and Anne Pusey (2004) report three further intercommunity attacks observed at Gombe, and one finding of a dead adolescent male who had apparently been killed by other chimpanzees. All the attacks were perpetrated by parties of males who appeared to have deliberately ranged beyond their usual core territory in search of individuals from neighbouring communities. Two of the observed attacks led to the death of an infant, the third to the severe wounding of a young male. They occurred in 1993 and 1998. Observations were suspended during 2000 and

Chagnon's work on the Yanomamö has played an important role in the advocacy of such an approach to human violence. It was Chagnon's ethnography of the Yanomamö that provided Wrangham and Peterson with the evidence for their claim for a direct link between human and chimpanzee 'warfare'. Chagnon's study, originally subtitled *The fierce people* (Chagnon 1968) and still (fifth edition) bearing a cover illustration of armed warriors, presents a vivid picture of pervasive warfare in a society on the borders of Brazil and Venezuela. Chagnon has also claimed evidence of an intrinsic link between warfare and natural selection. In 1988, he published data showing that *unokai* – Yanomamö men who had killed other men – reproduced more successfully than did non-killers. According to Wrangham and Peterson, *unokai* have 2.5 times the average number of wives as other men, and more than 3 times the average number of children as other men. This allowed Wrangham and Peterson to conclude 'lethal raiding among the Yanomamö, it seems, gives the raiders a genetic success' (Wrangham and Peterson 1996: 68). Wrangham and Peterson pose the rhetorical question: 'Is the elaborate . . . edifice of cerebral material that makes up our humanity still deeply infused with the essence of that ancient

2001 in case the chimpanzees were emboldened by the presence of humans, but the dead male was discovered in 2002. While the sample is small, Wilson, Wallauer and Pusey conclude that the age and sex of the victims support the hypotheses that the benefit of such incursions into neighbouring territories is to reduce the number of rival males, or to reduce competition for food in zones where the territories of adjacent communities overlap. They tend to reject the alternative hypothesis that infants are killed to induce the mother to defect to the attackers' community. Their approach is consistent with Aureli, Cords and Van Schaik (2002): 'such violence, like other forms of aggression, is a *strategic option* employed when assessment of expected *costs and benefits* indicates that attack will yield net benefits to the attackers' (Wilson, Wallauer and Pusey 2004: 524).

forest brain' embodied in the common ancestor of chimps and humans (Wrangham and Peterson 1996: 62)?

Christopher Boehm (1992) begins from a similar character-isation of chimpanzees, but draws his comparison more gener-ally with 'the warlike non-literate societies that feud' (Boehm 1992: 140). Among these he includes some hunter-gatherers but also the cattle-herding Nuer and the Tiv farmers of Africa, New Guinea horticulturalists and Montenegrin tribesmen in Europe (Boehm 1992: 154, 162). He argues these societies are all characterised, like chimpanzee communities, by patrilineal recruitment to groups and patrilocal residence. That is, peo-ple both belong to, and live with, their father's group. Boehm accepts that not all human hunter-gatherer societies defend the boundaries of their territories, and bases much of his dis-cussion on the hunting, herding and horticultural societies which best fit his model.

Violence and peacemaking

I argue that violence and peacemaking are both parts of a broader social complex. One cannot be discussed without the other. In the early 1970s, Jonathan Miller gave a sem-inar to the Anthropology Department at University College London about Sir Henry Head and W. H. Rivers's experiments on nerve regeneration, conducted after the First World War. Head and Rivers concluded that a primeval all-or-nothing nervous response was first restored, later to be overlain by a civilised, moderated reaction. Miller compared this to the notion that modern cars/automobiles possess a primeval, Model-T Ford accelerator, barely kept in check by sophisti-cated, modern brakes. As Miller pointed out, even the Model-T Ford required an integrated system of accelerator and brake in order to function effectively. According to Wrangham and

Peterson (1996: 64), the chimpanzee evidence shows that warfare is not an instrument of policy or a product of social conditions. 'The appetite for engagement, the excited assembly of a war party, the stealthy raid, the discovery of an enemy and the quick estimation of odds, the gang-kill, and the escape are common elements that *make intercommunity violence possible for both*' (Wrangham and Peterson 1996: 71, my emphasis). This is the 'primeval accelerator' approach.

A recent review article (Aureli, Cords and Van Schaik 2002) stresses that violence is costly for all social animals. Ways of placing a brake on violence are beneficial to all social species:

> For gregarious animals, conflict of interest, while unavoidable, may compromise the benefits of group living or neighbourliness, *especially when it escalates into aggression*. If this induces the losers to leave the group, they forfeit the benefits of group life, or face the risks associated with transfer into another group. The departure of the losers may also reduce the benefits of group living to the winners and, even without leaving, aggression may jeopardise future co-operation. Similar costs are likely in territorial species that have stable relations with neighbours. (Aureli, Cords and Van Schaik 2002: 325, my italics)

Filipo Aureli and his co-authors conclude: 'Behavioural mechanisms that mitigate conflicts, prevent aggressive escalation and resolve disputes should therefore be strongly selected in animals living in stable social organisations' (325). One example they cite in favour of this hypothesis is that male chimpanzees engage in reconciliations after conflict more frequently than do females (Aureli, Cords and Van Schaik 2002: 334). In other words, aggression risks depriving individuals of the benefits gained from a social relationship.

A potential objection to extending Aureli, Cords and Van Schaik's findings to human societies is that they are primarily concerned with relationships between members of the same local group. They do, however, argue 'similar costs are likely in territorial species that have stable relations with neighbours' (see above). In a paper written with my colleague Robert Barton (Layton and Barton 2001) we argue that a comparison of human and chimpanzee territoriality reveals that hunter-gatherers have developed flexible forms of territorial behaviour which generally circumvent the conditions that apparently lead to inter-group violence among chimpanzees. Chimpanzees live in social groups comparable in size to human hunter-gatherer bands (20–100 individuals), but chimpanzee groups are autonomous, whereas hunter-gatherers in low latitudes can move freely between bands within a larger regional community sustained by various forms of exchange. The regional community typically comprises about ten to fifteen bands, often totalling 500 people but sometimes numbering up to 1,500. This phenomenon is what Lars Rodseth et al. (1991) and Clive Gamble (1998) called 'the release from proximity', the emergence of social networks which *depend* on uniquely human genetic skills yet extend and transform the social environment into which the individual human is born (cf. Geertz 1973c).

What ecological pressures might have favoured the development of wider social networks among humans? Eric Alden Smith (1988) provided an explanation for the benefits to hunter-gatherers of being able to join different bands, or forage temporarily on the territory of another band. Smith argued that in many environments inhabited by hunter-gatherers, bands in a region would be uncertain about which area would contain the most abundant resources at any time, and would recognise resources fail in different territories at different times. This is particularly the case in the semi-arid tropical environments in which modern humans are thought to have evolved. If one band's territory experiences better rainfall than its neighbours, the band will benefit from allowing other bands to share its windfall, provided those bands in turn allow their former hosts to camp with them when the unpredictable sequence of rainfall favours the former guests. In these circumstances mutual access to each other's territories is an adaptive strategy. The patterns of inter-band visiting and gift exchange characteristic of hunter-gatherers function to maintain the regional network of social relationships upon which rights of mutual access depend. Even Chagnon (1988: 987) reports that Yanomamö lineages frequently move between villages and this, to some extent, inhibits raiding between villages containing recent allies.

Layton and Barton (2001) concluded that permeable territorial boundaries are most adaptive in a sparse, patchy and unpredictable environment (cf. Davies and Houston 1984, Dyson-Hudson and Smith 1978). Since most chimpanzees live in forest, whereas modern humans probably evolved in a savanna environment, we hypothesised that the genetic capability for sustaining social relationships that allow movement between bands evolved after the separation of the human and chimpanzee lines of evolution. We argued the patrilineal basis of many of the human societies cited by Boehm (1992) is ideological rather than actual. In other words, men may address each other as 'brother', but the actual composition of the coalition at the core of human local groups is, in practice (and unlike chimpanzees), rarely if ever exclusively a group of males biologically descended from a common ancestor (see chapter 2). The starting point for any comparison between humans and any non-human primate species must be the *behaviour* of both species, not the ideology of one and the behaviour of the other. Chimpanzee territorial behaviour cannot therefore be equated with the ancestral human pattern.

Since inter-group violence will threaten regional social networks, it is most likely to occur where little value is attached to such networks. Mutual access is least adaptive in environments where resources are dense and patchy, but seasonally predictable in distribution (the opposite of the scenario described by E. A. Smith). The best-documented exception to the right to forage on neighbouring band territories was found on the northwest coast of North America, where resources are densely distributed, and predictable in their seasonal abundance. Northwest coast territories were held, and their boundaries defended, by hunter-gatherer lineages. Trespassers were killed (Boas 1966: 35); land could be alienated and slaves taken during warfare (Garfield and Wingert 1966: 14, 29). This pattern was not a primeval one. Herbert Maschner (1997) dates the origin of northwest coast warfare to the period between AD 200 and AD 500, when the post-glacial sea level had stabilised and modern vegetation patterns become established.

In many small-scale human societies, inter-group conflict is more restrained than on the northwest coast. The anthropologist W. E. H. Stanner witnessed a 'large-scale fight' between two Australian Aboriginal groups in 1932. The men were arranged in two parties, one painted with white, the other with yellow pigment. They stood in two irregular lines, about sixty paces apart. Women ran into the midst of the combat to give their men further weapons. Despite the 'anger, challenge and derision' on both sides, there was also control. Only light duelling spears were in use. 'I saw one powerful aborigine, on what seemed the weaker side, run abruptly from the middle of the fight to wrestle fiercely with supporters to gain possession of the heavy, iron-bladed spears. They would not yield them, and sought to pacify him' (Stanner 1960: 65). Towards sunset, the battle ceased 'and some of the antagonists began to fraternise . . . No one had been mortally hurt though many had painful flesh wounds' (66). Several weeks later, Stanner attended an initiation ceremony. Both sides to the dispute were present. Even though they were 'at violent enmity . . . [the] bad feeling had been suppressed, after the aboriginal fashion, for a necessary tribal affair' (67). Stanner's vivid account gives an impression of the delicate counterbalancing of violence and peace that Aureli, Cords and Van Schaik's argument predicts (for a similar account of regulated conflict among the Yukpa of Venezuela, see Halbmayer 2001: 63). I therefore agree with Randall McGuire's review of warfare among the Pueblos of the southwest United States: 'People are not by nature either peaceful or warlike; some conditions lead to war, others do not' (McGuire 2002: 141).

HOW PROTOTYPICAL IS YANOMAMÖ WARFARE?

Evidence for the flexibility and situational aptness of warfare calls the typicality of the Yanomamö into question. Chagnon's depiction of the Yanomami came under intense scrutiny after the publication of Patrick Tierney's book *Darkness in El Dorado* (Tierney 2000). This book renewed debate on the 'naturalness' of warfare in simple human societies and highlighted a serious debate between sociobiology and cultural anthropology. Tierney, a journalist who had worked in the South American rain forest, interviewed anthropologists, missionaries and others who were familiar with Chagnon's work among the Yanomami. He noted that Chagnon's supervisor believed in the existence of genes for 'leadership' or 'innate ability' (Neel 1980). James Neel had argued that, in small-scale societies, male carriers of these genes would gain access to a disproportionate share of the available females, thus reproducing their own genes more frequently than less 'innately able' males. Tierney claimed Chagnon's work has been directed toward portraying the Yanomamö as exactly the kind of originary human society envisaged by Neel, displaying a Hobbesian state of savagery (cf. Chagnon 1988: 990). Tierney claims Chagnon had 'recooked' his data to fit sociobiological predictions and deliberately fomented conflicts between Yanomami as, for example, during Timothy Asch's films *The feast* and *The ax fight*, where (he alleges) artificial villages were used for sets (but see Biella 2000). Not only was Chagnon's work exploited by Venezuelan politicians and gold miners to justify massacres of Yanomami and expropriation of their land, Chagnon himself joined forces with corrupt politicians to gain control of Yanomami lands for illegal gold mining and continued anthropological access.

News of Tierney's book *Darkness in El Dorado* circulated, before its publication, through an email that Terry Turner and Leslie Sponsel sent to Louise Lamphere, President of the American Anthropological Association in late August 2000. The email was rapidly disseminated across the Internet. I will not try to give a comprehensive review here of the Yanomamö debate, but focus on issues of direct relevance to this chapter.

Sociobiology and cultural anthropology

The vehemence of Turner and Sponsel's email is an expression of a current debate in the United States between sociobiologists and cultural anthropologists. Among the most outspoken critics of cultural anthropology are the evolutionary psychologists Lida Cosmides and John Tooby (Cosmides, Tooby and Barkow 1992), who argue the human mind is endowed with complex, genetically determined skills that developed through natural selection during the long period our species lived by hunting and gathering (see chapter 3). According to Cosmides and Tooby, variation in human behaviour can be explained as the emergence of local adaptations predicated on the mind's inherent skills rather than – as social anthropologists might argue – cultural variation (see chapter 2). Tooby quickly jumped to Chagnon's defence (http://slate.msn.com/HeyWait/00-10-24/HeyWait.asp), and pointed out many inaccuracies in Tierney's citations (see also Ruby 2000). Tooby further pointed out that Turner and Sponsel were long-time adversaries of Chagnon (See Tooby's website http://www.psych.ucsb.edu/research/cep/eldorado/ witchcraft.html).

The dispute between evolutionary psychologists and cultural anthropologists is partly an issue concerning the preferred level of analysis. Cosmides and Tooby's primary targets are the French sociologist Emile Durkheim and the US anthropologist Clifford Geertz. Geertz is interested in culturally specific 'webs of significance'. His research method is dedicated to resolving the problems of interpretation posed by trying to understand an exotic culture's values, figures of speech and assumptions (e.g. Geertz 1973a, 1973b). If one wanted to understand the cultural significance of the head-dresses worn in Highland New Guinea during warfare and competitive feasting, for example, one would need to gain entry to culturally specific worlds of meaning, not examine the universal features of conflict.

There is, however, a more fundamental issue identified by Durkheim (1938 [1901]), that of the emergent properties of interaction (again, see chapter 2). As Michael Fischer comments,

What seems to infuriate cultural anthropologists about sociobiologists is their insistence on extrapolating from quite interesting statistics of animal mating and patterns of investment in care of offspring, and the various predictive models that can be made of these patterns, to the Vietnam War or the decisions of the Supreme Court. (Fischer 2001: 13)

Chapter 2 noted that evolutionary theorists debate whether the primary motor of evolution is the gene (Dawkins 1976), or the ecological system that exerts selective pressures on genetic variations in a population. Stuart Kauffman (1993) and Simon Conway Morris (1998) argue that the environment to which organisms adapt is transformed by the emergent properties of interaction. At least some of the cognitive skills cited by Tooby and Cosmides (language, co-operation) are only adaptive in a social environment, i.e. an environment characterised by the emergent properties of social interaction. Here, I believe, social anthropologists can validly criticise narrow theories of genetic causation that discount the way the environment that exerts selective pressures is constructed. The extent to which violence is adaptive will also depend at least partly on the socially constructed environment. The alleged adaptive significance of warfare among the Yanomami must be assessed in the context of the specific natural and social environment in which the Yanomami live.

Even if some people have a genetic predisposition to violence, this might not trigger co-ordinated social conflict. The question of whether social trends can be explained by scaling up from the intrinsic properties of the individual was another issue addressed by Durkheim. Durkheim (1952 [1897]) attacked the idea that suicide rates in late nineteenth-century France could be explained as waves of 'copycat' actions following an individual suicide. He argued that an increase or decrease in the suicide rate arose from the state of society. Durkheim postulated a range of personality types vulnerable to different kinds of suicide, ranging from the despair brought on by isolation, to giving one's life for the fatherland in the heat of battle. Durkheim argued that during periods of social disintegration the first type would be more vulnerable, but the second type would be most vulnerable during a period of intense patriotism. A similar issue is debated in a recent volume sponsored by the British Psycho-Analytical Society in response to the terrorist attacks of 11 September 2001. Does one have to study the psychology of the terrorist to explain the attack on the World Trade Center, or is it enough to posit a random range of personality types and study the social conditions that push some individuals into action? Among contributors to this debate, Renos Papadopoulos argues that psycho-analysts 'seem to have missed glaring external factors such as environmental pressures, socio-political realities, and historical legacies' (Papadopoulos 2002: 269). Stuart Twemlo and Frank Sacco go further, acknowledging that terrorism may be directed 'against the inadmissible perversion of a whole society' (Twemlo and Sacco 2002: 101).

Jürg Helbling proposed that the specific context of Yanomamö social behaviour encouraged violence. He argued that they are trapped in a form of the Prisoner's Dilemma that discourages the development of reciprocal altruism. Each lineage must convey the impression that they are 'tough guys' rather than trusting suckers. Further, if their partners in an exchange relationship betray them, the effect of military defeat would be so devastating that it would be too late to punish the partners by not reciprocating in the next round of the game, as many of the 'suckers' would be dead (Helbling 1999: 108–9). This creates a social environment that favours aggressive individuals. Alliances will only be sustained if both sides anticipate a long-term benefit, an outcome that is difficult to rely upon under such circumstances (Helbling 1999: 111).

Wrangham and Peterson claimed that 'no human society provides a better opportunity for comparison than the Yanomamö . . . because they have been so remarkably protected from modern political influences' (Wrangham and Peterson 1996: 64). One of Tierney's most valid criticisms is that the Yanomami were not representative of the original human condition when Chagnon studied them. Far from being 'uncontaminated' by contact with the outside world, they had interacted with outsiders since the eighteenth century, as victims of slave raiders, enemies of settlers and subjects of missionary endeavours. Fischer (2001) agrees that one of the most disconcerting aspects of writing about the Yanomamö is the way that their long history of contact with slavers, rubber tappers and others has sometimes been ignored.

The American Anthropological Association task force created to investigate Tierney's claims noted that Chagnon's 1988 *Science* paper (which reported that 44 per cent of Yanomamö men claimed to have killed someone) coincided with a disastrous moment in the Yanomami struggle for land rights, when the Brazilian president authorised the division of Yanomami land into reserves in order, it was claimed, to bring them under control. The Brazilian anthropologist Manuela Carneiro da Cunha pointed out in 1989 that Chagnon's paper had been widely reported in the popular press, both in Brazil and the United States. It is highly likely his arguments were damaging to the Yanomami, justifying violence against them, and Chagnon had not done enough to counter these negative images, despite toning down his language in later editions of his ethnography (American Anthropological Association 2002: 1.32–4).

Chagnon's data

In view of this controversy, it is important to re-examine Chagnon's original data. Chagnon (1988: 985) does not claim the existence of a gene for leadership, but he does claim that being a killer among the Yanomamö enhances one's reproductive success. Chagnon (1988: table 2) shows that those claiming *unokai* (killer) status undoubtedly have more children than non-*unokai*. *Unokai* average 4.91 children, non-*unokai* average 1.59 children. Compared across all adult age groups, *unokai* therefore do better than non-*unokai* by a ratio of 3:1 (Wrangham and Peterson's wording (1996: 68) misleadingly implies this is the difference between *unokai* and the *average* number of wives and children in the whole sample). Tierney (2000: 159) objects that Chagnon included unmarried men in his sample. In fact, Chagnon (1988: table 2) does not distinguish between unmarried and married men, but he does break down the figures into age groups. The figures supplied in Chagnon's table show that 94 per cent of men aged between twenty and twenty-four are non-*unokai*, but only 38 per cent of those aged forty-one and over. The status of *unokai* is achieved. Many non-*unokai* must either die young, or become *unokai* with age. Chagnon's sample of men aged twenty to twenty-four includes 5 *unokai* in a total of 83, while his sample of men over forty includes 75 *unokai* in a total of 121. This demonstrates many men who are not *unokai* between the ages of 20 and 24 can expect to achieve that status later in life. Chagnon asks whether becoming an *unokai* makes one more vulnerable to violent death and replies that it does not. 'Of 15 recent killings . . . nine of the males were under thirty years of age, their ages at death and the political histories of their respective villages at the time they were killed suggest that few, if any of them, were *unokai*' (990). Since only 14 per cent of men under thirty are *unokai*, this is not surprising.

A Yanomamö man reaches marriageable age in his early twenties (Chagnon 1997: 154). Table 2 in Chagnon 1988 supplies data on family size for men aged twenty onwards. Most of the young men who have just started to have children are non-*unokai*. The size of their families will inevitably be smaller than those of older men. Chagnon has therefore overestimated the advantage of being an *unokai* by combining data for incomplete and completed families. The most accurate measure of the advantage of being an *unokai* is to compare reproductive success among *unokai* and non-*unokai* over forty, where family size is most probably complete. *Unokai* over forty have an average of 6.99 children, non-*unokai* over forty have an average of 4.19. In other words, *Unokai* have 1.67 children for every 1 child born to a non-*unokai*. They are advantaged, but not to the extent implied by Chagnon's all-age ratio of 3:1. The advantage is, moreover, not sufficient to eliminate non-*unokai* from the population. Thirty-eight per cent of men over forty are non-*unokai*. If one were to make a narrow presumption of genetic causation, this would suggest some form of polymorphism (i.e. that there are also selective advantages to being a non-*unokai*). One does not need to assume narrow genetic causation to see that killing is not the whole story.

Approximately 30 per cent of deaths among adult males in the region of the Yanomamö tribe are due to violence (Chagnon 1988: 986), but 44 per cent of living men aged twenty-five or older claim to have killed someone (987). That means either that a proportion (32 per cent) of claimed killings must be spurious or, at least, that more than one person has been responsible for the same killing. 'Many victims are shot by just one or two raiders, but one victim was shot by 15 members of the raiding party' (Chagnon 1988: 987). Chagnon (1988: fig. 1) documents the number of victims for whom living killers *unokaied*. He notes that 60 per cent (83 of 137) claim to have participated in only one killing while, at the other extreme, one man claims to have participated in sixteen different killings. A small proportion of men stand out as multiple killers (two claim fourteen killings each, another two claim twelve). Seventy-five per cent of claimed killings (more than enough to account for the level of reported deaths) are accounted for by the fifty-five *unokai* who reported having killed two or more men. These fifty-five constitute a mere 16 per cent of the adult male population. For most men, the aim is probably simply to have a reputation for fierceness (see Halbmayer 2001: 62 on the Yukpa of northwestern Venezuela). Tierney points out that very few women are actually abducted among the Yanomamö. Even Chagnon's low figure of 17 per cent is higher than that recorded elsewhere among the Yanomamö, and some of these were probably willing elopements (Tierney 2000: 159–64). It is curious that, even though 30 per cent of Yanomamö men get killed in fighting, Chagnon still claims there is a shortage of marriageable women (Chagnon 1997: 157).[2]

Warfare and territoriality

The Yanomamö reportedly say inter-village warfare does not take place over resources (Wrangham and Peterson 1996: 66). Although Chagnon denies that Yanomamö warfare is for territorial gain, he writes: 'Where the Yanomamö have bordered the territory of other peoples they have fought with them and consistently pushed them out . . . and have virtually exterminated the Makú Indians' (Chagnon 1967: 129). It seems clear there is a territorial dimension to Yanomamö warfare (cf. Helbling 1999: 106), and that it is not solely motivated by the quest for wives. In general, the population densities of human hunter-gatherers are very low compared with other primates. It is populations living at high densities that are prone to boundary defence and its corollary, cross-boundary raiding, which may result in deaths. Inter-group warfare is well

---

[2] Are more than 30 per cent of Yanomami girls the victims of infanticide? Chagnon says he has not published on infanticide since 1985, in order to protect the Yanomamö from prosecution, but he has never observed a case of infanticide (1997: 94).

documented on the northwest coast of North America (Rosman and Rubel 1971) which was noted above as an exception to the common pattern of flexible territoriality among hunter-gatherers. A good case has recently been made for its former existence in western Arnhem Land, north Australia (Taçon and Chippindale 1994), at a time that coincided with the flooding of low-lying land when sea levels rose after the last glacial period. In both cases, population density is exceptionally high for recent hunter-gatherers (nortwest coast: 0.4 to 0.67/km², coastal Arnhem Land: 0.3–0.5/km²). The central Yanomamö were reported to have a density of 0.34 persons/kilometre² (Lizot 1977: 122), which falls within this range.

Warfare and mating

Why might adult men among the Yanomamö fall into two categories, 'killers' and 'non-killers'? The 'group selection' fallacy was mentioned in chapter 2. *If* social behaviour is genetically determined, individuals who forgo their own reproductive interests to benefit others will not transmit their altruistic genes to the next generation. Altruism will be displaced by selfishness. When altruistic behaviour is genetically determined, it can only persist if it enhances the bearer's reproductive success. Could this be the case among Yanomamö? The two theories concerning the evolution of altruism were summarised in chapter 2. One argues that altruism will be favoured by natural selection if the fortunate recipient of an altruistic act carries the same gene as the altruist who makes the sacrifice. This is known as kin selection. The alternative theory is that, if the giver and receiver have a continuing social relationship, the altruist will receive help from the other at a later date. This is known as reciprocal altruism. It is represented in Axelrod's model for the evolution of co-operation, and exemplified by the rights of mutual access to territories between hunter-gatherer bands in uncertain environments. 'Free-riders' are those who accept resources without reciprocating (see chapter 2), while the victim of non-reciprocation is a 'sucker'.

In his analyses of Yanomamö behaviour, Chagnon (1982) is explicit in his intention to explore the explanatory power of a kin-selecting model, but his data suggest that reciprocal altruism may also play a part in structuring behaviour toward socially recognised kin, despite the high risk noted by Helbling (1999) in his application of game theory to Yanomamö behaviour. Competition for spouses among the Yanomamö is reduced by a form of reciprocal altruism. A pair of men in different groups agree to exchange their sisters so that each can have a wife (Chagnon 1979), and this alliance can be perpetuated by further marriage exchanges. Yanomamö marriage strategies are based on the distinction between parallel and cross cousins. Parallel cousins (children of the father's brother and mother's sister) belong to one's own lineage. Cross cousins (children of the father's sister and mother's brother) belong to the lineage with whom one's father exchanged sisters (see Figure 2.1, p. 60). Cross cousins are ideal marriage partners if an alliance is to be extended. Parallel cousins are classed as 'sister' or 'brother', cross cousins as 'wife' or 'brother-in-law'. The latter terms are extended to other members of an allied lineage. Forty per cent of Yanomami marriages are between people *culturally classified as cross cousins*, but who are not in fact first cousins. Chagnon recognises that culturally based (rather than genetic) distinctions between parallel and cross cousins are crucial to marriage exchange (Chagnon 1982: figs. 14.12–13; Chagnon 1979). Use of the kinship terminology, according to which a man calls women of his own lineage 'sister', and those of an allied lineage 'wife', can therefore be regarded as a signal of commitment to continued reciprocal, altruistic exchange between two groups. This level of social organisation is definitely not found in chimpanzee communities, and is based on the unique capacity of humans to construct inter-group relations.

Chagnon claims that the age difference between men and women at marriage creates different generation lengths of men and women and frequently requires the rules to be broken if marriage practices are to work (1997: 154). This is a common problem in classificatory kinship systems (see Keen 1982 for an example from Australia). It is more likely that, as Chagnon illustrates (1997: 147), rules are subject to competing interpretations rather than broken. When a particular classification no longer reflects political expediency, the leader of a Yanomami lineage takes the initiative in signalling lineage fission. He does so by reclassifying distant 'sisters' (distant parallel cousins) as 'wives' (Chagnon 1979). Chagnon subtitled his 1982 paper 'Man the rule breaker'. But to conclude that man is more of a rule breaker than a rule maker does not tell us who makes the rules (or why).

An alternative vision of Yanomamö society might go as follows. Horticultural societies are particularly vulnerable to warfare because they have dense patches of desirable resources (their garden crops), but lack an overarching social organisation to regulate inter-village access to gardens peacefully. A precarious form of reciprocal altruism is therefore negotiated around marriage exchanges that seek to guarantee order, a good example of Adam Ferguson's concept of civil society in the 'state of nature'. But this order is repeatedly undermined by free-riders who organise raids or split large lineages to their personal advantage, while jeopardising the lives of others. Villages that split may become enemies (Chagnon 1988: 987, 988), and small villages are more vulnerable to attack than large ones (Chagnon 1988: 986). Promoting raids may bring short-term gains, but undermine longer-term social relationships. If Yanomamö men can loosely be divided into 'killers' and 'peacemakers', this would reflect the precarious balance between the two competing strategies in their social life.

THE BROADER PICTURE ON WARFARE IN SMALL-SCALE SOCIETIES

If we want to understand when and why human warfare began, it seems that we need to look at the emergent properties of social and ecological systems. Layton and Barton (2001) hypothesised that human warfare first occurred when hunter-gatherers moved into environments with dense and predictable resources. In the areas of the world best studied archaeologically, this would have occurred in post-glacial times, during the Mesolithic. The cultural invention of farming, creating defended fields of dense crops, will have exacerbated the trend. Carol and Melvin Ember (1997) found that hunter-gatherer societies were not particularly peaceful, but had a lower frequency of war than non-foragers. They also found that victors in those societies that fight at least once every two years almost always take land or other resources from the defeated. Land is less likely to be at issue among hunter-gatherers that allow mutual access to each other's territory.

Warfare originated on the northwest coast of North America as a consequence of change in the natural ecology. The coast has been inhabited since 9000 BC, but during the long period between 9000 and 3500 BC groups were small and mobile (Maschner 1997). At that time, unstable sea levels precluded the development of dense, predictable food resources. The first evidence for conflict on the northwest coast occurs by

3000 BC, coinciding with evidence for more stable foraging movement in the form of shell middens, and is seen primarily in non-lethal skeletal injuries. Herb Maschner cautions that violent conflict may have occurred earlier, without generating archaeological evidence. From AD 200–500, however, the onset of warfare is evident in the construction of defensive sites, the amalgamation of what may have been single lineage communities into large villages and population decline. The bow and arrow were introduced to the region at that time. 'The wars that did result in changes in territory, at least in every recorded case, were the result of expansionist activities by the most populous and strongest group in a region, and the group that had the greatest amount of subsistence resources in their own territory' (Maschner 1997: 292). Those with least territory had neither the wealth nor the numbers to undertake a successful attack.

Paul Sillitoe (1978) examined the role of Big Men in warfare in New Guinea. Big Men are not simply strong men who can push others around; while admired as skilful organisers and talkers, they must respect the Melanesian principle that all men are equal and free to control their own affairs. Here is another example of Adam Ferguson's civil society in the state of nature. Big Men's scope for political action depends on the flexibility of local social organisation, and the extent to which it allows disaffected individuals to join influential leaders in other villages. Big Men fear the encroachment of rivals and try to use force to sustain or extend their own influence. Insecure Big Men are more likely to foment discord (Sillitoe 1978: 265 and table 4). Sillitoe distinguishes between minor wars that punish a breakdown in reciprocity between groups who regularly trade and exchange marriage partners, and deep-rooted wars that persist between groups that lack such interrelationships but seek constantly to revenge past killings by the enemy (compare Halbmayer 2001: 59, 61 on South America). Routing the enemy is more popular in major wars between settlements not normally linked by exchange. 'There is a good chance a war [of redress] . . . will end in the rout of the defeated and the pillage of their settlement' (Sillitoe 1978: 263).

Sillitoe notes that different types of military engagement tend to be found in different New Guinea environments. Swamp and dense rain forest support a lower density of population, so there are both fewer occasions for people to meet and less scope for Big Men to construct inter-community networks. Sillitoe rejects a simple correlation between population pressure and frequent war (Sillitoe 1978: 269; see also Sillitoe 1977), but it is clear that war for territorial conquest is most prevalent in certain environments.

VIOLENT CONFLICT IN COMPLEX SOCIETIES

Chapter 2 noted that anthropologists prefer to address theoretical issues through analysis of the simplest human societies, where the fundamental aspects of social life can most clearly be seen. The applicability of their conclusions to complex societies needs to be demonstrated. Among horticulturalists, warfare arises from broken alliances between neighbouring villages, or irresolvable conflict between socially unrelated groups. In complex societies, many recent ethnic conflicts have been associated with instability in the nation state. The question here is, what factors lead to the collapse of large-scale social networks? Chapter 3 showed that the breakdown of social order rarely if ever results in total anarchy or lack of social interaction. When the existing social order does break down, ethnicity and kinship are two key dimensions on which to reconstruct trust, but on a smaller scale, between people who interact and claim exclusive rights to resources. Kinship and ethnicity are not primordial forms of social organisation that resurface during periods of anarchy. They are called upon where they have continued to be salient aspects of government or civil society. What parallels can be drawn with warfare among the Yanomamö? Rather than accepting Wrangham and Peterson's argument that we are confronted with a primordial lust for 'the excited assembly of a war party, the stealthy raid, the discovery of an enemy and the quick estimation of odds, the gang-kill' (Wrangham and Peterson 1996: 71), I argue the parallel lies in the construction and opportunistic repudiation of social relationships. Two similarities stand out: the conflict of interest between those who benefit from order and disorder, and the role of outsiders in supplying weapons that increase the destructive impact of conflict.

Who has an interest in promoting disorder?

Albanian blood feuds are brought to an end by creating classificatory brotherhood between the groups. Both parties must agree that honour has been satisfied. Clan leaders (*bajraktars*) acted as judges, who arbitrated in disputes. The Ottoman Turks relied on them heavily (Whitaker 1968: 259). In northern Albania, traditional leaders, local Catholic priests, and a national mission led by Pjetr Ndreki have all helped to settle blood feuds during the 1990s. However, Stephanie Schwandner-Sievers reports that younger men (in their forties and fifties), who were born under Communism, are unfamiliar with the traditional rituals of reconciliation and are unwilling to accept them (140). Many of this generation are also involved in trading drugs, weapons and women between Albania, Montenegro, Kosovo and Italy. There are fortunes to be made in trading illegal drugs; therefore it is in the interest of gangs to prevent the restoration of state control. In Sierra Leone, groups of bandits in pursuit of loot and diamonds imitate rebel tactics, making it harder to establish peace negotiations (Richards 1996: 7, 132).

Stephen Handelman (1994) argues that the rise of the black market in Russia during the 1960s increased the power of criminal gangs that had existed for many decades. During the Chubais privatisation programme, introduced under President Yeltsin, gangs gained control of black market trade and co-operated with local state officials with whom they shared an interest in weakening central control over the economy. After privatisation, a number of criminal cartels became linked to high government officials, who used organised crime groups to empower their struggle for control of the industries, banks etc. that once belonged to the state. 'The Russian gang is arguably the only Soviet institution that benefited from the collapse of the USSR' (Handelman 1994: 87). In 1997, the Russian parliament voted by 288 to 6 that privatisation had been unsatisfactory. Fifty-seven per cent of Russia's firms were privatised, but the state only received $3–5 billion, because the firms had been sold at nominal prices to corrupt cliques who had an interest in sustaining disorder in civil society.

The role of outsiders

Fighting among the Yanomamö may partly be caused by competition for trade goods (Ferguson 1995, Fischer 2001: 10 and Helbling 1999: 105). There is plausible evidence that Chagnon's selective provision of machetes increased the severity of raiding among the Yanomamö. Tierney argued that Chagnon provoked warfare by distributing machetes and other metal goods to win the favour of Yanomami from whom he needed to collect blood samples and genealogies. The desire for steel implements drew Yanomami from other villages toward Chagnon, allowing disease to spread and thus stoking claims of sorcery. These claims were supported to some extent by the findings of the American Anthropological Association's Task Force. The Task Force report quotes a Yanomami spokesperson, José Seripino, who told a member of the force, 'In those days we didn't have our own motors and he came with all that material – his research materials. The Yanomami needed these things – we were getting them from peasants. So one community has them and another not. Then other communities will get "fighting mad" (Spanish *bravo*)' (American Anthropological Association 2002: 2.97–8, parenthesis in original).

Wrangham and Peterson (1996: 77) claim that violent deaths among the !Kung (Ju/'hoansi) hunter gatherers of the Kalahari are more frequent than in America's worst cities. Richard Lee (1979: 382), the leading authority on the Ju/'hoansi, estimates there were twenty-two instances of homicide among Dobe Ju/'hoansi in the thirty years between 1920 and 1955. In 1964 the population, including temporary residents, was 466, while in 1968 it was 584 (Lee 1979: 43). Fifteen killings arose in the course of feuds, while seven were single killings that did not provoke retaliation. Five deaths were prompted by marital disputes, but at least five victims were innocent bystanders (Lee 1979: 383, 389). While this may seem a high death rate, the homicide rate rose considerably between 1978 and 1980. In just three years there were seven cases of Ju/'hoansi killing other Ju/'hoansi, often in drunken brawls. Murders increased because men were now using weapons issued by the South African army during their war with Namibian nationalist guerrillas (Lee and Hurlich 1982: 341).

The evidence that many recent wars afflicting nation states have been rendered more deadly by the introduction of powerful weapons supplied by other nations is overwhelming. Traditional procedures for resolving disputes may be unequal to the greater scale of destruction. Firearms were introduced into northern Albania during Ottoman Turkish rule, which made feuding much easier and more lethal (Schwandner-Sievers 1999: 146). While unable to provide precise dates, Schwandner-Sievers quotes sources who deduce that muskets were introduced to neighbouring Montenegro in about 1700, and 'modern' firearms (i.e. breech-loading rifles) in about 1820. In 1907 an Austrian nobleman carried out a survey of deaths in thirty villages over a period of fifteen years, and calculated that 19 per cent of deaths arose from feuding.

Keebet von Benda-Beckmann (2004), writing on recent violence on the Indonesian island of Ambon, notes that some of the contemporary violence resembles a traditional pattern of violent conflict management. If, for instance, a close relative is wounded in a traffic accident, brothers and cousins set out to catch the presumed perpetrator. If found, he will be beaten severely, perhaps even killed. If the alleged perpetrator is not found, negotiation and reconciliation can be undertaken by elderly relatives. Now, however, the traditional social restrictions that previously restrained serious escalation seem to be failing. During the first month of the conflict reviewed in chapter 3 only knives and home-made weapons were used. Imported guns and automatic weapons have since increased the level of violence to a previously unknown level. The community to be defended has expanded from relatives and the village to the entire religious community. The elderly no longer know whom to talk to, or how to re-create peace. The staff of rural mosques are locally appointed and do not belong to a hierarchy beyond the village level, while Christian church organisation is not embedded in *adat* (traditional law). There is, therefore, no clear basis on which to re-establish mutual trust.

In Africa, huge quantities of lethal weapons have increased violence; arms control is very difficult (Ferguson 2003: 5). In nineteenth-century Somalia the most lethal weapon was the spear, but in 1992 'every man and youth I encountered was very visibly armed with a Kalashnikov, or American equivalent, and there appeared to be plenty of heavy weapons in the background' (Lewis 1997: 184). There was also a lively trade in tanks across the Ethiopian border. Somalia was armed first by the Soviet Union and later by the United States. As clan authority in Somalia broke down during the 1980s, competition among urban elites was often played out along genealogical lines, *but without the constraining rules of customary law* (Besteman, 2003: 292, my emphasis).

At the start of civil war in Chad, in 1966, 'there were almost no fighters, nothing to fight with, and no way to get to the fight' (Reyna 2003: 279). The Frolinat rebels had perhaps a hundred partisans fighting with lances, while President Tombalbaye had a thousand soldiers armed with antiquated rifles and light machine guns. By Habré's rule in 1986–7, 'there were perhaps 20,000 soldiers in different liberation armies armed with everything from tanks, to missiles, to phosphorus mortars. Habré may have had up to 25,000 people in his army' (Reyna 2003: 276–7). There has, as Steve Reyna (277) puts it, been 'a spectacular accumulation of the means of violence in postcolonial Chad'. Many states have been involved, but particularly France, Libya and the United States.

The restoration of trust

If the breakdown of mutual trust can also be interpreted as the consequence of moving from a non-zero-sum game to a zero-sum game, then peace could be restored by persuading opponents that they can both benefit from the cessation of conflict. If this is so, they have an incentive to negotiate peace (compare chapter 2 on the threat of mutual destruction in nuclear war).

In northern Somalia peace was restored in 1991. Locally based Somali clans were able, without outside help, to rebuild peace. They were encouraged by the potential economic benefits of restoring safe travel in search of pasture and safe trade routes. David Pratten also shows how effectively local communities in East Africa can draw on traditional forms of social organisation to combat anarchy and oppression (Pratten 1997 and 2000).

Peace negotiations can be based on a complex assessment of the relative costs and benefits of alternative plans, in the search for a Nash equilibrium. Opponents may be persuaded to accept a compromise that represents the most feasible route to settled co-existence (Barakat et al. 2001: 177). Sultan Barakat and his co-authors describe the negotiations they undertook to rebuild a formerly Muslim village in Bosnia that had been colonised by Bosnian Croats during the civil war of the 1990s. The most feasible solution for allowing settled co-existence between the two parties entailed both sides making compromises. It was agreed that the Muslim refugees would return to their homes and rebuild the mosque in return for handing properties above the current water supply level to the Croats, who would then benefit from a new water supply taking water to higher ground. External agencies can thus play a part by making co-operation a precondition for assistance (see also Leutloff-Grandits 2003). The critical issue concerns the distribution of power between those who see benefit in the restoration of order, and those who, like the Yanomami *unokai*, benefit from disorder.

CONCLUSION

Order and anarchy began as an enquiry into why social change sometimes proceeds in an orderly fashion while at other times society disintegrates into disorder and civil war. One possible explanation – advocated by Thomas Hobbes and Napoleon

Chagnon – is that humans are inherently prone to violence, and will only renounce warfare when the state, or some other arbiter, can guarantee everyone will adhere to their social obligations. If the state weakens, anarchy results. Another possibility – championed by John Locke and Adam Ferguson – is that humans have always been capable of building co-operation and reciprocity through recognition that social order is in their long-term self-interest. The scope of social relations, however, fluctuates according to the extent to which mutual trust can be relied upon, or wellbeing increased through joint action. The case studies analysed here support the latter explanation. Social change can undermine trust and deprive people of needed resources. Trust is a fragile resource. Where free-riding brings high rewards (as in the Johannesburg gold rush) people may decide they can dispense with mutual obligations. Where resources are fixed, where others' trustworthiness is doubtful, individuals may sever extensive social ties to acknowledge only members of a village, kin group or ethnic community, often one that asserts a superior right to scarce resources.

Civil society is made up of the relations people construct among themselves, out of self-interest. I do not discount the possibility that men and women may act through disinterested altruism, but it is more persuasive to start from the 'bottom line' – that self-interest must be satisfied if social relations are to persist. Competition and exploitation are as important in human society as are co-operation and mutual aid. Whether civil society is considered a 'good thing', or not, depends both on the character of the social order and the stand-point of the person passing judgement. Those who believe society should consist of individual entrepreneurs will advocate a different kind of civil society to those who believe that mutual aid is the key to human welfare. Where the state is oppressive, civil society can play a valuable role in promoting human rights. Where a multi-ethnic state is experiencing economic hardship, factionalism in civil society can destroy the lives of many citizens.

Chapter 4 has looked at the Yanomamö case in detail because I believe it illustrates some fundamental points about evolutionary approaches to human social behaviour. Charles Darwin's theory of evolution emphasised variability and contingency: variability in behaviour within a population, and contingency in environments. Even if aggression and warfare bring benefits to individual Yanomami men, this does not justify the conclusion that warfare is in any universal sense adaptive. Not all Yanomami men are 'killers', and those who seek such a reputation take advantage of the particular instability of Yanomami alliances that stems from the difficulty of sustaining trust between villages. From a global perspective, the success of one supposed personality type in one specific social environment is less important than is (as Durkheim suggested in his study of suicide) a general understanding of the relative outcomes of different social strategies in different circumstances.

The arguments for a direct evolutionary link between chimpanzee inter-group aggression and human warfare are simplistic. Humans differ from chimpanzees in their ability to construct social relationships on a wider scale, with individuals beyond the local band. Humans have evolved a greater capacity for learning and for keeping track of multiple social relations. These skills, seen clearly in the cultural interpretation of kinship, do not free humans from the constraints of natural selection, but they do allow us to respond more flexibly and with greater innovation to the challenges of social life. There is undoubtedly a genetic component in our ability to keep track of the state of reciprocal relationships. The evolution of the brain can be matched to the size of social groups among primates, i.e. apes and monkeys (Dunbar 1993), but the environment to which such a condition is adaptive is largely socially constructed. Peacemaking skills have evolved in concert with the importance of social relationships among primates (de Waal 1989).

Human warfare arises when the web of social relationships is compromised. Human societies are complex systems and vulnerable to periods of disorder. The more unstable the state of the system, the greater the probability that a small, chance event will deflect it along a new historical trajectory (Stewart 1997: 127–9). It is at such moments that selfish leaders or unscrupulous mass media, as in Yugoslavia and Rwanda, have maximum opportunity to change the course of history. In periods of uncertainty, people are willing to accept as leader anyone who offers a simple and quick solution, however inept that solution subsequently proves to be. Once people can foresee the end of mutual dependence within a wider society, they may abandon reciprocal obligations and seek to re-establish relations within a more exclusive group. Warfare can be intensified by the supply of lethal weapons, sometimes beyond the level that can be handled by local procedures for reconciliation. The manipulative activities of leaders play a part in fomenting war, whether they are local Big Men in small-scale, uncentralised societies, or the leaders of nation states. Leaders, however, can only manipulate social relationships constructed and sustained, or repudiated, by the communities within which they operate.

Our species evolved in a social environment. As Adam Ferguson put it in 1767: 'Mankind are to be taken in groupes, as they have always subsisted' (Ferguson 1995: 10). *Order and anarchy* has argued against the view that the capitalist market economy is uniquely conducive to the creation of civil society. Chapter 1 showed that Locke and Ferguson, the originators of the concept, regarded civil society as much more widely applicable. Historical and recent, non-Western examples were given in support of Locke's and Ferguson's position. The book has therefore argued that 'civil society' should include all those social organisations occupying the space between the household and the state that enable people to co-ordinate their management of resources and activities. It has done so in order to explore the usefulness of Locke's and Ferguson's original conceptualisations of civil society, in which people pursue social relations out of rational self-interest in all types of society, ranging from humankind's 'natural' condition (in politically uncentralised societies) to the nation state. This approach is justified by demonstrating the applicability of the same analytical models (game theory, the Prisoner's Dilemma) to social interaction in both simple and complex societies.

In this broader approach to civil society, no presumption is made concerning the contribution that civil society makes to coherence in the state, nor are some human societies treated as 'more evolved' than others. Civil society may support or undermine the unity of the nation state, depending on historical circumstances. Rationality is not seen as unique to social action in market democracies. While it is entirely reasonable to search for forms of civil society that promote co-operation and order throughout the state, it is unhelpful to label those that do not do so as 'primordial' or 'irrational'. Their situational rationality must be investigated, even if the violence they promote is condemned.

The narrow conceptualisation of civil society on which Seligman (1992) and Gellner (1994) relied implies that traditional social institutions such as kinship and ethnic groups are irrational and therefore followed blindly. Since allegiances to kin or ethnic identities seemed intellectually inexplicable, the only remedy appeared to be to introduce a universal market economy, dissolve traditional communities and thus infuse behaviour with rationality. In practice, misguided implementation of the principles defended by Seligman and Gellner has promoted social disorder rather than coherence. Failure to understand the rationality of other forms of society makes it harder to anticipate the consequences of social change. Privatisation of common land held by local communities has enabled the rise of a landowning elite and, more importantly, has destroyed the traditional local civil society. Local people are dispossessed of productive resources and become vulnerable to exploitation by potential patrons. We should rather explore the rationality of allegiance to kin and ethnic communities in specific social contexts.

Violence is not inevitable, not an uncontrollable genetically programmed trait inherited from the common ancestor of humans and chimpanzees, but a response to particular conditions in the ecology of society. The desire to promote order is equally entrenched in our behaviour. The wider approach advocated here makes it possible to understand why it is in some people's interests to promote a wider social order, but in others' interests to disrupt it. Socially disruptive actions are sometimes, from the actor's perspective, rational, and civil war is not treated as an outbreak of irrationality, but as a reasoned response to particular social conditions. The aim of this book has not been to defend violence but to explain the conditions that compromise society and cause morally reprehensible behaviour, as much as it has been to understand the origins of social order. It has also sought to demonstrate that inter-ethnic violence and feuding between kin groups in distant parts of the world are precipitated by changes in the ecology of global society, an ecology in which we also participate and which is shaped by the policies of our own governments.

References

Abélès, M. 1991. *Quiet days in Burgundy: a study in local politics*, trans A. McDermott, Cambridge: Cambridge University Press (French edition 1989).

Abrahams, R. 1990. 'Chaos and Kachin', *Anthropology Today*, 6: 15–17.

Albrecht. 1937. Letter to Deputy Administrator Alice Springs, quoted in Australian National Archives file AA: CRS A659 40/1/1428, 'Suggestions re Aboriginal Reserves in south-west of Northern Territory, January 1935–May 1940'.

Alderdice, Lord. 2002. 'Introduction', in C. Covington, P. Williams, J. Arundale and J. Knox (eds.), *Terrorism and war: unconscious dynamics of political violence*, London: Karnac Books, pp. 1–16.

Allen, R. C. 1991. 'The two English agricultural revolutions, 1459–1850', in B. M. S. Campbell and M. Overton (eds.), *Land, labour and livestock: historical studies in European agricultural production*, Manchester: Manchester University Press, pp. 236–54.

Amanor, K. S. 1999. 'Global restructuring and land rights in Ghana', Research Report no. 108, Uppsala: Nordiska Afrikainstitutet.

American Anthropological Association. 2002. *The El Dorado task force report*. http://www.aaanet.org/edtt/final/preface.htm

Ardrey, R. 1967. *The territorial imperative: a personal enquiry into the animal origins of property and nations*, London: Collins.

Ault, W. O. 1972. *Open-field farming in medieval England: a study of village by-laws*, London: Allen and Unwin.

Aureli, F., M. Cords and C. P. Van Schaik. 2002. 'Conflict resolution following aggression in gregarious animals: a predictive framework', *Animal Behaviour*, 64: 325–43.

Axelrod, R. 1990. *The evolution of co-operation*, Harmondsworth: Penguin (first published in 1984 by Basic Books, New York).

Bailey, F. G. 1969. *Stratagems and spoils: a social anthropology of politics*, Oxford: Blackwell.

Banks, M. 1999. 'Ethnicity and reports of the 1992–95 Bosnian conflict', in T. Allen and J. Seaton (eds.), *The media of war*, London: Zed Books, pp. 147–61.

Barakat, S., C. Wilson, V. Simcic and M. Kojakovic. 2001. 'Challenges and dilemmas facing the reconstruction of war-damaged cultural heritage: the case of Pocitelj, Bosnia-Herzegovina', in R. Layton, P. Stone and J. Thomas (eds.), *Destruction and conservation of cultural property*, London: Routledge, pp. 168–81.

Barth, F. 1959. 'Segmentary opposition and the theory of games', *Journal of the Royal Anthropological Institute*, 89: 5–21.

1969. 'Introduction', in F. Barth (ed.), *Ethnic groups and boundaries: the social organization of culture difference*, London: Allen and Unwin, pp. 9–38.

Basalla, G. 1988. *The evolution of technology*, Cambridge: Cambridge University Press.

Beattie, J. 1961. 'Democratisation in Bunyoro', *Civilizations*, 11.1: 8–20, reprinted in J. Middleton (ed.), *Black Africa today*, London: Macmillan, pp. 101–10 (page references are to the reprint).

Behar, R. 1986. *Santa María del Monte: the presence of the past in a Spanish village*, Princeton: Princeton University Press.

Benda-Beckmann, F. von. 1990. 'Sago, law and food security on Ambon', in J. I. H. Bakker (ed.), *The world food crisis: food security in comparative perspective*, Toronto: Canadian Scholars' Press Inc., pp. 157–99.

2001. 'Between free riders and free raiders: property rights and soil degradation in context', in N. Heerink, H. van Keulen and M. Kuiper (eds.), *Economic policy analysis and sustainable land use: recent advances in quantitative analysis for developing countries*, Heidelberg: Physica Verlag, pp. 293–316.

Benda-Beckmann, F. von and K. von Benda-Beckmann. 1999. 'A functional analysis of property rights, with special reference to Indonesia', in T. van Meijl and F. von Benda-Beckmann (eds.), *Land and natural resources in southeast Asia and Oceania*, London: Kegan Paul International, pp. 15–56.

Benda-Beckmann, K. von. 2004. 'Law, violence and peace making on the island of Ambon', in M.-C. Foblets and T. von Trotha (eds.), *Healing the wounds: essays on the reconstruction of societies after war*, Oxford: Hart.

Berlin, I. 2002. *Freedom and its betrayal: six enemies of human liberty*, London: Random House.

Besteman, C. 2003. 'The Cold War and chaos in Somalia', in R. B. Ferguson (ed.), *The state, identity and violence: political disintegration in the post-Cold War world*, London: Routledge, pp. 285–99.

Biella, P. 2000. 'Visual anthropology in the plague year: Tierney and the Yanomamö films of Asch and Chagnon', *Anthropology News*, December: 5–6.

Blau, P. 1964. *Exchange and power in social life*, New York: Wiley.

Bloch, M. 1966. *French rural history: an essay on its basic characteristics*, trans. J. Sondheimer, London: Routledge (French edition 1931).

Boas, F. 1888. 'The central Eskimos', *Bureau of American Ethnology, Annual Report*, 6: 399–699.

 1966. *Kwakiutl ethnography*, ed. H. Codere, Chicago: Chicago University Press.

Boehm, C. 1992. 'Segmentary "warfare" and the management of conflict: comparison of East African chimpanzees and patrilineal–patrilocal humans', in A. H. Harcourt and F. B. M. de Waal (eds.), *Coalitions and alliances in humans and other animals*, Oxford: Oxford University Press, pp. 137–73.

Bohannan, L. 1958. 'Political aspects of Tiv social organisation', in J. Middleton and D. Tait (eds.), *Tribes without rulers*, London: Routledge, pp. 33–66.

Bourdieu, P. 1977. *Outline of a theory of practice*, trans. R. Nice, Cambridge: Cambridge University Press (French edition 1972).

Bowden, M. 1999. *Black Hawk down*, London: Bantam.

Boyd, R. and P. J. Richerson. 1985. *Culture and the evolutionary process*, Chicago: University of Chicago Press.

Brain, C. K. 1981. *The hunters or the hunted? An introduction to African cave taphonomy*, Chicago: Chicago University Press.

Buchowski, M. 1996. 'The shifting meanings of civil and civic society in Poland', in C. Hann and E. Dunn (eds.), *Civil society: challenging Western models*, London: Routledge, pp. 79–98.

Burch, E. 1975. *Eskimo kinsmen: changing family relationships in northwest Alaska*, New York: West.

Burrow, J. W. 1981. *A liberal descent: Victorian historians and the English past*, Cambridge: Cambridge University Press.

Cam, H. M. 1962. *Law-finders and law-makers in medieval England*, London: Methuen.

Campbell, J. K. 1964. *Honour, family and patronage*, London: Oxford University Press.

Chagnon, N. 1967. 'Yanomamö social organisation and warfare', in M. Fried, M. Harris and R. Murphy (eds.), *War: the anthropology of armed conflict and aggression*, New York: Natural History Press, pp. 109–59.

1968. *Yanomamö: the fierce people*, New York: Holt, Rinehart and Winston.

1979. 'Mate competition, favouring close kin, and village fissioning among the Yanomamö Indians', in N. Chagnon and W. Irons (eds.), *Evolutionary biology and human social behaviour*, North Scituate, Mass.: Duxbury, pp. 86–132.

1982. 'Sociodemographic attributes of nepotism in tribal populations: man the rule breaker', in King's College Sociobiology Group (eds.), *Current problems in sociobiology*, Cambridge: Cambridge University Press, pp. 291–318.

1988. 'Life histories, blood revenge and warfare in a tribal population', *Science*, 239: 985–92.

1997. *Yanomamö*, fifth edn., Fort Worth: Harcourt Brace.

Chapman, B. 1953. *Introduction to French local government*, London: Unwin.

Chibnall, A. C. 1965. *Sherington: fiefs and fields of a Buckinghamshire village*, Cambridge: Cambridge University Press.

Conway Morris, S. 1998. *The crucible of creation: the Burgess Shale and the rise of animals*, Oxford: Oxford University Press.

Cosmides, L., J. Tooby and J. Barkow. 1992. 'Introduction: evolutionary psychology and conceptual integration', in J. H. Barkow, L. Cosmides and J. Tooby (eds.), *The adapted mind: evolutionary psychology and the generation of culture*, New York: Oxford University Press, pp. 4–136.

Dart, R. 1925. '*Australopithicus africanus*: the man-ape of South Africa', *Nature*, 115: 195–9.

1959. *Adventures with the missing link*, London: Hamilton.

Davies, N. B. 1981. 'Calling as an ownership convention on pied wagtail territories', *Animal Behaviour*, 29: 529–34.

Davies, N. B. and A. I. Houston. 1984. 'Territory economics', in J. R. Krebs and N. B. Davies (eds.), *Behavioural ecology: an evolutionary approach*, Oxford: Blackwell, pp. 148–69.

Dawkins, R. 1976. *The selfish gene*, Oxford: Oxford University Press.

Day, T. E. 1916. *Examination of the country west of the Overland Telegraph Line*, Northern Territory Bulletin no. 20, Department of Homes and Territories, Melbourne (Australian National Archives file CRS A3, item 22/2391).

Declich, F. 2001. '"When silence makes history": gender and memories of war violence in Somalia', in B. Schmidt and I. Schröder (eds.), *Anthropology of violence and conflict*, London: Routledge, pp. 161–75.

Denich, B. 1994. 'Dismembering Yugoslavia: nationalist ideologies and the symbolic revival of genocide', *American Ethnologist*, 21: 367–90.

2003. 'The specter of superfluity: genesis of schism in the dismantling of Yugoslavia', in R. B. Ferguson (ed.), *The state, identity and violence: political disintegration in the post-Cold War world*, London: Routledge, pp. 177–98.

Doja, A. 1999. 'Morphologie traditionelle de la société Albanaise', *Social Anthropology*, 7: 421–38.

Duffield, M. 1981. *Maiurno: capitalism and rural life in Sudan*, Sudan Studies Series no. 5, London: Ithaca Press.

1994. 'The political economy of internal war', in J. Macrae and A. Zwi (eds.), *War and hunger*, London: Zed Books, pp. 50–69.

2001. *Global governance and the new wars: the merging of development and security*, London: Zed Books.

Dunbar, R. 1993. 'Co-evolution of neocortical size, group size and language in humans', *Behavioural and Brain Sciences Evolution*, 16: 681–735.

Dunn, E. 1996. 'Money, morality and modes of civil society among American Mormons', in C. Hann and E. Dunn (eds.), *Civil society: challenging Western models*, London: Routledge, pp. 27–49.

Durham, W. H. 1991. *Co-evolution: genes, culture and human diversity*, Stanford: Stanford University Press.

Durkheim, E. 1938. *The rules of sociological method*, trans. S. A. Solovay and J. H. Mueller, London: Macmillan (French edition 1901).

1952. *Suicide: a study in sociology*, trans. J. Spaulding and G. Simpson, London: Routledge and Kegan Paul (French edition 1897).

Dyson-Hudson, R. and E. A. Smith. 1978. 'Human territoriality: an ecological assessment', *American Anthropologist*, 80: 21–41.

Eames, E. 1990. 'Navigating Nigerian bureaucracies', in J. P. Spradley and D. W. McCurdy (eds.), *Conformity and conflict: readings in cultural anthropology*, 7th edn., Glenview, Ill.: Scott, Foresman, pp. 38–47 (first published 1985).

Eidson, J. and G. Milligan. 2003. 'Cooperative entrepreneurs? Collectivization and privatization of agriculture in two East German regions', in C. Hann and the 'Property Relations' Group (eds.), *The postsocialist agrarian question: property relations and the rural condition*, Münster: LIT, pp. 47–92.

Elster, J. 1983. *Explaining technical change*, Cambridge: Cambridge University Press.

Ember, C. R. and M. Ember. 1997. 'Violence in the ethnographic record: results of cross-cultural research on war and aggression', in D. L. Martin and D. W. Frayer (eds.), *Troubled times: violence and warfare in the past*, Amsterdam: Gordon and Breach, pp. 1–20.

Epstein, A. L. 1958. *Politics in an urban African community*, Manchester: Manchester University Press, for the Rhodes-Livingstone Institute.

Erasmus, C. J. 1956. 'Culture, structure and process: the occurrence and disappearance of reciprocal farm labour in Latin America', *Southwestern Journal of Anthropology*, 12: 444–69.

Evans-Pritchard, E. E. 1940. *The Nuer*, Oxford: Clarendon Press.

Fabian, J. 1983. *Time and the other*, New York: Columbia University Press.

Fairhead, J. 2000. 'The conflict over natural and environmental resources', in F. Stewart, W. Nafziger and R. Vayryen (eds.), *War, hunger and displacement*, vol. 1, Oxford: Oxford University Press, pp. 147–78.

Fallers, L. 1956. *Bantu bureaucracy*, Cambridge: W. Heffer, for the East African Institute of Social Research.

Ferguson, A. 1995. *An essay on the history of civil society*, Cambridge: Cambridge University Press (first published 1767).

Ferguson, R. B. 1995. *Yanomami warfare*, Santa Fe, N.M.: School of American Research.

2003. 'Introduction: violent conflict and the control of the state', in R. B. Ferguson (ed.), *The state, identity and violence: political disintegration in the post-Cold War world*, London: Routledge, pp. 1–58.

Fischer, M. 2001. 'In the science zone: the Yamomami and the fight for representation', *Anthropology Today*, 17.4: 9–14. Concluding section in *Anthropology Today*, 17.5: 16–19.

Foucault, M. 1977. *Discipline and punish: the birth of the prison*, London: Penguin.

Friedl, J. 1974. *Kippel: a changing village in the Alps*, New York: Holt, Rinehart.

Gallagher, T. 1997. 'My neighbour, my enemy: the manipulation of ethnic identity and the origins and conduct of war in Yugoslavia', in D. Turton (ed.), *War and ethnicity: global connections and local violence*, Rochester, N.Y.: University of Rochester Press, pp. 47–75.

Gamble, C. 1998. 'Palaeolithic society and the release from proximity: a network approach to intimate relations', *World Archaeology*, 29: 426–49.

Garfield, V. and P. Wingert. 1966. *The Tsimshian Indians and their arts*, Seattle: University of Washington Press.

Garwood, A. 2002. 'The Holocaust and the power of powerlessness: survivor guilt an unhealed wound', in C. Covington, P. Williams, J. Arundale and J. Knox (eds.), *Terrorism and war: unconscious dynamics of political violence*, London: Karnac Books, pp. 353–74.

Geertz, C. 1973a. 'Thick description: towards an interpretive theory of culture', in C. Geertz, *The interpretation of cultures*, London: Hutchinson, pp. 3–30.

1973b. 'Deep play: notes on the Balinese cock fight', in C. Geertz, *The interpretation of cultures*, London: Hutchinson, pp. 412–53.

1973c. 'The growth of culture and the evolution of mind', in C. Geertz, *The interpretation of cultures*, London: Hutchinson, pp. 55–83.

Gellner, E. 1994. *Conditions of liberty: civil society and its rivals*, Harmondsworth: Penguin (page references are to the 1996 edition).

Ghiglieri, M. P. 1984. *The chimpanzees of Kibale Forest: a field study of ecology and social structure*, New York: Columbia University Press.

Giddens, A. 1984. *The constitution of society*, Cambridge: Polity Press.

Glazier, N. and D. P. Moynihan. 1979. 'Why ethnicity?' in D. R. Colburn and G. E. Pozzatta (eds.), *America and the new ethnicity*, Port Washington, N.Y.: National University/Kennikat Press, pp. 29–42.

Glickman, M. 1971. 'Kinship and credit among the Nuer', *Africa*, 41: 306–19.

Goddard, C. 1987. *A basic Pitjantjatjara/Yunkunytjatjara to English dictionary*, Alice Springs: Institute of Aboriginal Development.

Goldschmidt, W. 1979. 'A general model for pastoral social systems', in Equipe Ecologique (ed.), *Pastoral production and society*, Cambridge: Cambridge University Press, pp. 15–28.

Goodall, J. 1986. *The chimpanzees of Gombe: principles of behaviour*, Cambridge, Mass.: Harvard University Press.

Goody, J. 1956. 'A comparative approach to incest and adultery', *British Journal of Sociology*, 7: 286–305.

2001. 'Civil society in an extra-European perspective', in S. Kaviraj and S. Khilnani (eds.), *Civil society: history and perspectives*, Cambridge, Cambridge University Press, pp. 149–64.

Gouldner, A. 1980. 'Civil society in capitalism and socialism', in A. Gouldner, *The two Marxisms*, London: Macmillan, pp. 355–73.

Gournay, B., J. F. Kesler and J. Siwek-Pouydesseau. 1967. *Administration publique*, Paris: Presses Universitaires de France.

Grabher, G. and D. Stark. 1998. 'Organizing diversity: evolutionary theory, network analysis and post-socialism', in J. Pickles and A. Smith (eds.), *Theorising transition: the political economy of postcommunist transformations*, London: Routledge, pp. 54–75.

Grätz, T. 2002. *Gold mining communities in northern Benin as semiautonomous social fields*, Haale/Saale: Max Planck Institute for Social Anthropology, working paper no. 36.

Gunder Frank, A. 1971. *Capitalism and underdevelopment in Latin America: historical studies of Chile and Brazil*, Harmondsworth: Penguin.

Halbmayer, E. 2001. 'Socio-cosmological contexts and forms of violence: war, vendetta, duels and suicide among the Yukpa of north-western Venezuela', in B. Schmidt and I. Schröder (eds.), *Anthropology of violence and conflict*, London: Routledge, pp. 49–75.

Hamilton, W. D. 1964. 'The genetical evolution of social behaviour (I and II)', *Journal of Theoretical Biology*, 7: 1–52.

Hampson, N. 1963. *A social history of the French Revolution*, London: Routledge.

Handelman, S. 1994. 'The Russian mafiya', *Foreign Affairs*, 73.2: 83–96.

Hann, C. M. 1990. 'Second economy and civil society', in C. M. Hann (ed.), *Market economy and civil society in Hungary*, London: Frank Cass, pp. 21–44.

2003. 'Civil society: the sickness, not the cure?' *Social Evolution and History*, 2.2: 34–54.

Hardin, G. 1968. 'The tragedy of the commons', *Science*, 162: 1243–8.

Havinden, M. A. 1961. 'Agricultural progress in open-field Oxfordshire', *Agricultural History Review*, 9: 73–83.

Helbling, J. 1999. 'The dynamics of war and alliance among the Yanomami', in G. Elwert, S. Feuchtwang and D. Neubert (eds.), *Dynamics of violence: processes in escalation and de-escalation of violent group conflicts*, Berlin: Duncker and Humblot, pp. 103–15.

Hill, C. 1958. *Puritanism and revolution*, London: Secker and Warburg.

Hilton, R. H. 1962. 'Peasant movements in England before 1381', in E. M. Carus-Wilson (ed.), *Essays in economic history*, vol. 2, London: Arnold, pp. 73–90.

Hobbes, T. 1970. *Leviathan, or the matter, form, and power of a commonwealth, ecclesiastical and civil*, London: Dent (first published 1651).

Hobbs, D., P. Hadfield, S. Lister and S. Winlow. 2003. *Bouncers: violence and governance in the night time economy*, Oxford: Oxford University Press.

Hobsbawm, E. 1992. 'Ethnicity and nationalism in Europe today', *Anthropology Today*, 8.1: 3–8.

Hobsbawm, E. and T. Ranger (eds.). 1983. *The invention of tradition*, Cambridge: Cambridge University Press.

Hoebel, E. A. 1954. *The law of primitive man*, Cambridge, Mass.: Harvard University Press.

Holden, C. and R. Mace. 2003. 'Spread of cattle led to the loss of matri-lineal descent in Africa: a coevolutionary analysis', *Proceedings of the Royal Society, London*, 270: 2425–33.

James, W. 2002. 'The anthropological family: from ancestors to affines', Presidential Address distributed with *Anthropology Today*, 18.6.

Jansen, S. 1998. 'Homeless at home: narrations of post-Yugoslav iden-tities', in A. Dawson and N. Rapport (eds.), *Migrant identities: perceptions of 'home' in a world of movement*, Oxford: Berg, pp. 85–109.

—— 2000. 'Victims, rebels, underdogs: discursive practices on resistance in Serbian protest', *Critique of Anthropology*, 20: 393–419.

Kaplan, H. and K. Hill. 1985. 'Food sharing among Ache foragers: tests of explanatory hypotheses', *Current Anthropology*, 26: 223–46.

Kaplan, H., K. Hill and A. M. Hurtado. 1990. 'Risk, foraging and foodsharing among the Ache', in E. Cashdan (ed.), *Risk and uncertainty in tribal and peasant economies*, Boulder, Colo.: West-view, pp. 107–43.

Kaplan, R. D. 1994. 'The coming anarchy: how scarcity, crime, over-population, and disease are rapidly destroying the social fabric of our planet', *Atlantic Monthly*, February: 44–76.

Kauffman, S. 1993. *The origins of order: self-organisation and selection in evolution*, Oxford: Oxford University Press.

Keen, I. 1982. 'How some Murngin men marry ten wives', *Man*, 17: 620–42.

Kemp, S. 1932. *Black frontiers: pioneer adventures with Cecil Rhodes' mounted police in Africa*, London: Harrap.

Khilnani, S. 2001. 'The development of civil society', in S. Kaviraj and S. Khilnani (eds.), *Civil society: history and perspectives*, Cambridge: Cambridge University Press, pp. 1–13.

Kingston-Mann, E. 1999. *In search of the true west: culture, economics, and problems of Russian development*, Princeton: Princeton University Press.

—— 2003. 'Deconstructing the romance of the bourgeoisie: a Russian Marxist path not taken', *Review of International Political Economy*, 10: 93–117.

Kropotkin, P. 1972. *Mutual aid: a factor in evolution*, New York: New York University Press (first published 1902).

Kumar, K. 1993. 'Civil society: an enquiry into the usefulness of an historical term', *British Journal of Sociology*, 44: 374–95.

Laland, K. and G. Brown. 2002. *Sense and nonsense: evolutionary perspectives on human behaviour*, Oxford: Oxford University Press.

Lambert, R. 1953. 'Structure agraire et économie rurale de plateau de Levier', *Bulletin de l'Association des géographes français*, 237–38: 170–8.

Laslett, P. 1960. 'Introduction', in J. Locke, *Two treatises of government*, Cambridge: Cambridge University Press, pp. 3–122.

Latouche, R. 1938. 'La fruitière jurasienne au XVIIIième siecle', *Revue de geographie alpine*, 26: 773–91.

Layton, R. 1986. *Uluru: an Aboriginal history of Ayers Rock*, Canberra: Aboriginal Studies Press.

1989. 'Are sociobiology and social anthropology compatible? The significance of sociocultural resources in human evolution', in R. Foley and V. Standen (eds.), *Comparative socioecology: the behavioural ecology of humans and other mammals*, Oxford: Blackwell, pp. 433–55.

1995. 'Relating to the country in the Western Desert', in E. Hirsch and M. O'Hanlon (eds.), *The anthropology of landscape: perspectives on place and space*, Oxford: Clarendon Press, pp. 210–31.

1997. *An introduction to theory in anthropology*. Cambridge: Cambridge University Press.

2000. *Anthropology and history in Franche Comté: a critique of social theory*, Oxford: Oxford University Press.

2003. 'Agency, structuration and complexity', in A. Bentley and H. Maschner (eds.), *Complex systems and archaeology*, Salt Lake City: University of Utah Press, pp. 103–9.

Layton, R. and R. Barton. 2001. 'Warfare and human social evolution', in K. Fewster and M. Zvelebil (eds.), *Ethnoarchaeology and hunter-gatherers: pictures at an exhibition*, BAR International Series 955, Oxford: Archaeopress, pp. 13–24.

Layton, R., P. Stone and J. Thomas (eds.). 2001. *Destruction and conservation of cultural property*, London: Routledge.

Leach, E. R. 1954. *Political systems of highland Burma*, London: Bell.

Lebeau, R. 1951. 'Deux anciens genres de vie opposés de la montagne jurassienne', *Revue de géographie de Lyon*, 26: 378–410.

Lee, R. B. 1979. *The !Kung San: men, women and work in a foraging society*, Cambridge: Cambridge University Press.

Lee, R. B. and S. Hurlich. 1982. 'From foragers to fighters: South Africa's militarization of the Namibian San', in E. Leacock and R. B. Lee (eds.), *Politics and history in band societies*, Cambridge: Cambridge University Press, pp. 327–45.

Lem, W. 1999. *Cultivating dissent: work, identity and praxis in rural Languedoc*, New York: State University of New York Press.

Lessinger, J. 2003. '"Religious" violence in India: Ayodhya and the Hindu right', in B. R. Ferguson (ed.), *The state, identity and violence: political disintegration in the post-Cold War world*, London: Routledge, pp. 149–76.

Leutloff-Grandits, C. 2003. 'Coping with economic devastation: agriculture in post-war Knin, Croatia', in C. Hann and the 'Property Relations' Group (eds.), *The postsocialist agrarian question: property relations and the rural condition*, Münster: LIT, pp. 143–70.

Lévi-Strauss, C. 1966. *The savage mind*, London: Weidenfeld and Nicolson (French edition 1962).

 1969. *The elementary structures of kinship*, trans. J. H. Bell and J. R. von Sturmer, London: Eyre and Spottiswoode (French edition 1967).

 1973. *Tristes tropiques*, trans. J. and D. Weightman, London: Cape (French edition 1955).

Lewis, I. M. 1997. 'Clan conflict and ethnicity in Somalia: humanitarian intervention in a stateless society', in D. Turton (ed.), *War and ethnicity: global connections and local violence*, Rochester, N.Y.: University of Rochester Press, pp. 179–201.

Little, K. 1966. 'The political system of the Poro', *Africa*, 35: 349–65 and 36: 62–71.

Lizot, J. 1977. *Tales of the Yanomami*, Cambridge: Cambridge University Press.

Lloyd, W. F. 1964. 'The checks to population', in G. Hardin (ed.), *Population, evolution and birth control*, San Francisco: Freeman, pp. 337–42 (first published 1833).

Locke, J. 1960. *Two treatises of government*, Cambridge: Cambridge University Press (first published 1689).

Lorenz, K. 1966. *On aggression*, trans. M. Latzke, London: Methuen (German edition 1963).

MacDougall, H. A. 1982. *Racial myth in English history*, London: University Press of New England.

Malinowski, B. 1954. *Magic, science and religion*, New York: Doubleday.

Manson, J. H. and R. W. Wrangham. 1991. 'Intergroup aggression in chimpanzees and humans', *Current Anthropology*, 32: 369–90.

Marshall, L. 1957. 'The kin terminology of the !Kung Bushmen', *Africa*, 27: 1–25.

    1976. 'Sharing, talking and giving: relief of social tensions among the !Kung', in R. B. Lee and I. deVore (eds.), *Kalahari hunter-gatherers: studies of the !Kung San and their neighbours*, Cambridge, Mass.: Harvard University Press, pp. 350–71.

Mary-Rousselière, G. 1984. 'Iglulik', in D. Damas (ed.), *Handbook of North American Indians*, vol. 5, *Arctic*, Washington, D.C.: Smithsonian Institution, pp. 431–46.

Maschner, H. 1997. 'The evolution of northwest coast warfare', in D. L. Martin and D. W. Frayer (eds.), *Troubled times: violence and warfare in the past*, Amsterdam: Gordon and Breach, pp. 267–302.

Maynard Smith, J. 1982. *Evolution and the theory of games*, Cambridge: Cambridge University Press.

McAdam, D., S. Tarrow and C. Tilly. 2001. *Dynamics of contention*, Cambridge: Cambridge University Press.

McCay, B. and J. M. Acheson. 1987. *The question of the commons: the culture and ecology of communal resources*, Tucson: University of Arizona Press.

McGuire, R. 2002. 'Stories of power, powerful tales: a commentary on ancient Pueblo violence', in M. O'Donovan (ed.), *The dynamics of power*, Centre for Archaeological Investigations, occasional paper 30, Carbondale: Southern Illinois University, pp. 126–47.

Mendras, H. and A. Cole. 1991. *Social change in modern France: towards a cultural anthropology of the Fifth Republic*, Cambridge: Cambridge University Press.

Migdal, J. S. 1988. *Strong societies and weak states*, Princeton: Princeton University Press.

Nasar, S. 1998. *A beautiful mind*, London: Faber.

Neel, J. 1980. 'On being headman', *Perspectives in Biology and Medicine*, 23: 277–93.

Neeson, J. M. 1993. *Commoners: common right, enclosure and social change in England, 1700–1820*, Cambridge: Cambridge University Press.

Nelson, R. and S. Winter. 1982. *An evolutionary theory of economic change*, Cambridge, Mass.: Harvard University Press.

Netting, R. McC. 1981. *Balancing on an Alp: ecological change and continuity in a Swiss mountain community*, Cambridge: Cambridge University Press.

Neumann, J. von and O. Morgenstern. 1944. *Theory of games and economic behaviour*, Princeton: Princeton University Press.

Newby, H., C. Bell, D. Rose and P. Saunders. 1978. *Property, paternalism and power: class and control in rural England*, London: Hutchinson.

Nishida, T. 1979. 'The social structure of chimpanzees in the Mahale Mountains', in D. A. Hamburg and E. R. McCown (eds.), *The great apes*, Menlo Park, Calif.: Benjamin/Cummings, pp. 73–122.

Nishida, T., M. Haraiwa-Hasegawa and Y. Takahata. 1985. 'Group extinction and female transfer in wild chimpanzees in the Mahale National Park, Tanzania', *Zeitschrift für Tierpsychologie*, 67: 284–301.

Nishida, T., H. Takasaki and Y. Takahata. 1990. 'Demography and reproductive profiles', in T. Nishida (ed.), *The chimpanzees of the Mahale Mountains: sexual and life history strategies*, Tokyo: University of Tokyo Press, pp. 64–97.

Nowak, M. A. and K. Sigmund. 1998. 'Evolution of indirect reciprocity by image scoring', *Nature*, 393 (11 June): 573–7.

Nugent, D. 1982. 'Closed systems and contradiction: the Kachin in and out of history', *Man* (NS), 17: 508–27.

Orwin, C. S. and C. S. Orwin. 1938. *The open fields*, Oxford: Clarendon Press.

Ostrom, E. 1990. *Governing the commons: the evolution of institutions for collective action*, Cambridge: Cambridge University Press.

Overton, M. 1996. *Agricultural revolution in England: the transformation of the agrarian economy 1500–1850*, Cambridge: Cambridge University Press.

Panter-Brick, C. 1993. 'Seasonal organisation of work patterns', in S. J. Ulijaszek and S. S. Strickland (eds.), *Seasonality and human ecology*, Cambridge: Cambridge University Press, pp. 220–34.

Papadopoulos, R. 2002. 'Destructiveness, atrocities and healing: epistemological and clinical reflections', in C. Covington, P. Williams, J. Arundale and J. Knox (eds.), *Terrorism and war: unconscious dynamics of political violence*, London: Karnac Books, pp. 289–314.

Peters, C. M., A. H. Gentry and R. O. Mendelsohn. 1989. 'Valuation of an Amazonian rainforest', *Nature*, 339: 655–6.

Plumb, J. H. 1990. *England in the eighteenth century*, Harmondsworth: Penguin (first published 1950).

Pottier, J. 1996. 'Relief and repatriation: views by Rwandan refugees; lessons for humanitarian aid workers', *African Affairs*, 95: 403–29.

2001. *Re-imagining Rwanda: conflict, survival and disinformation in the late twentieth century*, Cambridge: Cambridge University Press.

Pratten, D. 1997. 'Local institutional development and relief in Ethiopia: a Kire-based seed distribution programme in North Wollo', *Disasters*, 21: 138–54.

2000. *Return to the roots? Urban networks, rural development and power in Sudan*, University of Edinburgh, Centre of African Studies Occasional Paper 82.

Radcliffe-Brown, A. R. 1952. *Structure and function in primitive society*, London, Cohen and West.

Rao, N. and C. R. Reddy. 2001. 'Ayodhya, the print media and communalism', in R. Layton, P. Stone and J. Thomas (eds.), *Destruction and conservation of cultural property*, London: Routledge, pp. 139–56.

Renfrew, C. 1978. 'Trajectory discontinuity and morphogenesis: the implications of Catastrophe Theory for archaeology', *American Antiquity*, 43: 203–21.

Reyna, S. P. 2003. 'A Cold War story: the barbarization of Chad (1966–91)', in R. B. Ferguson (ed.), *The state, identity and violence: political disintegration in the post-Cold War world*, London: Routledge, pp. 261–84.

Richards, P. 1996. *Fighting for the rain forest: war, youth and resources in Sierra Leone*, London: International African Institute. (Page references are to the 1999 edition.)

Ridley, M. 1996. *The origins of virtue*, London: Viking.

Rodseth, L., R. W. Wrangham, A. M. Harrigan and B. B. Smuts. 1991. 'The human community as a primate society', *Current Anthropology*, 32: 221–54.

Rosenberg, H. G. 1988. *A negotiated world: three centuries of change in a French alpine community*, Toronto: University of Toronto Press.

Rosman, A. and P. G. Rubel. 1971. *Feasting with mine enemy: rank and exchange among northwest coast societies*, New York: Columbia University Press.

Rousseau, J. J. 1963. *The social contract and discourses*, ed. G. D. H. Cole, London: Dent (first published 1755).

Ruby, J. 2000. 'Tierney's claims about Tim Asch', *Anthropology News*, December: 7.

Sahlins, M. 1974. *Stone age economics*. London: Tavistock.
   1976. *The use and abuse of biology: an anthropological critique of sociobiology*, Ann Arbor: University of Michigan Press.

Sampson, S. 1996. 'The social life of projects: importing civil society to Albania', in C. Hann and E. Dunn (eds.), *Civil society: challenging Western models*, London: Routledge, pp. 121–42.

Schlee, G. 2002. 'Regularity in chaos: the politics of difference in the recent history of Somalia', in G. Schlee (ed.), *Imagined differences: hatred and the construction of identity*, Münster: LIT, pp. 251–80.
   2004. 'Taking sides and constructing identities: reflections on conflict theory', *Journal of the Royal Anthropological Institute* (NS), 10: 135–56.

Schwandner-Sievers, S. 1999. 'Humiliation and reconciliation in Northern Albania: the logics of feuding in symbolic and diachronic perspectives', in G. Elwert, S. Feuchtwang and D. Neubert (eds.), *Dynamics of violence: processes in escalation and de-escalation of violent group conflicts*, Berlin: Duncker and Humblot, pp. 133–52.

Scott, J. 1976. *The moral economy of the peasant: rebellion and subsistence in Southeast Asia*, New Haven: Yale University Press.

Seligman, A. 1992. *The idea of civil society*, Princeton: Princeton University Press.

Sillitoe, P. 1977. 'Land shortage and war in New Guinea', *Ethnology*, 16: 71–81.
   1978. 'Big Men and war in New Guinea', *Man* (NS), 13: 252–71.

Smith, A. and J. Pickles. 1998. 'Introduction: theorising transition and the political economy of transformation', in J. Pickles and A. Smith (eds.), *Theorising transition: the political economy of post-communist transformations*, London: Routledge, pp. 1–22.

Smith, E. A. 1988. 'Risk and uncertainty in the "original affluent society": evolutionary ecology of resource-sharing and land tenure', in T. Ingold, J. Woodburn and D. Riches (eds.), *Hunters and gatherers: history, evolution and social change*, Oxford: Berg, pp. 222–51.

Song, M. 2003. *Choosing ethnic identity*, Cambridge: Polity Press.

Spencer, H. 1972. *Herbert Spencer on social evolution: selected writings*, ed. J. D. Y. Peel, Chicago: University of Chicago Press.

Spencer, P. 1965. *The Samburu: a study of gerontocracy in a nomadic tribe*, London: Routledge.

Spülbeck, S. 1996. 'Anti-semitism and fear of the public in a post-totalitarian society', in C. Hann and E. Dunn (eds.), *Civil society: challenging Western models*, London: Routledge, pp. 64–78.

Stanner, W. E. H. 1960. 'Durmugan, a Nangiomeri', in J. Casagrande (ed.), *In the company of man*, New York: Harper, pp. 64–100.

Stewart, I. 1997. *Does God play dice? The new mathematics of chaos*, Harmondsworth: Penguin.

Swain, N. 1992. *Hungary: the rise and fall of feasible socialism*, London: Verso.

Taçon, P. and C. Chippindale. 1994. 'Australia's ancient warriors', *Cambridge Archaeological Journal*, 4: 211–48.

Tanner, M. 1997. *Croatia: a nation forged in war*, New Haven: Yale University Press.

Taylor, C. 1999. *Sacrifice as terror: the Rwandan genocide of 1994*, Oxford: Berg.

Tester, K. 1992. *Civil society*, London: Routledge.

Tierney, P. 2000. *Darkness in El Dorado*, New York: Norton.

Tilly, C. 1981. *As sociology meets history*, New York: Academic Press.

Trivers, R. 1985. *Social evolution*, Menlo Park, Calif.: Benjamin/Cummins.

Turton, D. 1997. 'Introduction: war and ethnicity', in D. Turton (ed.), *War and ethnicity: global connections and local violence*, Rochester, N.Y.: University of Rochester Press, pp. 1–45.

Twemlo, S. and F. Sacco. 2002. 'Reflections on the making of a terrorist', in C. Covington, P. Williams, J. Arundale and J. Knox (eds.), *Terrorism and war: unconscious dynamics of political violence*, London: Karnac Books, pp. 97–123.

Tylor, E. 1903. *Primitive culture*, 4th edn., London: Murray.

Valen, L. van. 1973. 'A new evolutionary law', *Evolutionary Theory*, 1: 1–30.

Verderey, K. 1999. *The political lives of dead bodies*, New York: Columbia University Press.

Verdon, M. 1982. 'Where have all the lineages gone? Cattle and descent among the Nuer', *American Anthropologist*, 84: 566–79.

Viazzo, P. P. 1989. *Upland communities*, Cambridge: Cambridge University Press.

Vickery, W. L., L.-A. Giraldeau, J. Templeton, D. Kramer and C. Chapman. 1991. 'Producers, scroungers, and group foraging', *American Naturalist*, 137: 847–63.

Vucho, A. 'Beyond bombs and sanctions', in C. Covington, P. Williams, J. Arundale and J. Knox (eds.), *Terrorism and war: unconscious dynamics of political violence*, London: Karnac Books, pp. 51–67.

Vulliamy, E. 1994. *Seasons in Hell: understanding Bosnia*, London: Simon and Schuster.

Waal, A. de. 1989. *Famine that kills*, Oxford: Clarendon Press.

Waal, F. de. 1989. *Peacemaking among primates*, Cambridge, Mass.: Harvard University Press.

Wallerstein, I. 1974. *The modern world-system*, New York: Academic Press.

Weber, M. 1947. *The theory of social and economic organisation*, trans. A. R. Henderson and T. Parsons, London: Hedge and Co. (first published 1925).

Wedel, J. R. 1998. *Collision and collusion: the strange case of Western aid to Eastern Europe 1989–1998*, New York: St. Martin's Press.

Whitaker, I. 1968. 'Tribal structure and national politics in Albania', in I. M. Lewis (ed.), *History and social anthropology*, London: Tavistock, pp. 253–93.

White, J. 1996. 'Civic culture and Islam in urban Turkey', in C. Hann and E. Dunn (eds.), *Civil society: challenging Western models*, London: Routledge, pp. 143–53.

Wilson, D. and C. Game. 1994. *Local government in the United Kingdom*, Basingstoke: Macmillan.

Wilson, M., W. Wallauer and A. Pusey. 2004. 'New cases of intergroup violence among chimpanzees in Gombe National Park, Tanzania', *International Journal of Primatology*, 25: 523–49.

Winterhalder, B. 1996. 'Social foraging and the behavioural ecology of intragroup resource transfers', *Evolutionary Anthropology*, 5.2: 46–57.

Wrangham, R. and D. Peterson. 1996. *Demonic males: apes and the origins of human violence*, London: Bloomsbury.

Zubaida, S. 2001. 'Civil society, community, and democracy in the Middle East', in S. Kaviraj and S. Khilnani (eds.), *Civil society: history and possibilities*, Cambridge: Cambridge University Press, pp. 232–49.

Index

For EU product safety concerns, contact us at Calle de José Abascal, 56–1°,
28003 Madrid, Spain or eugpsr@cambridge.org.

www.ingramcontent.com/pod-product-compliance
Ingram Content Group UK Ltd.
Pitfield, Milton Keynes, MK11 3LW, UK
UKHW012345130625
459647UK00009B/544